Nombre: _____   Fecha: _____

W9-AHF-292

4 Saludos y despedidas

Look at the people in the drawing. Based on what you know about gestures of native Spanish speakers when greeting, circle only the number of the illustrations that are culturally authentic.

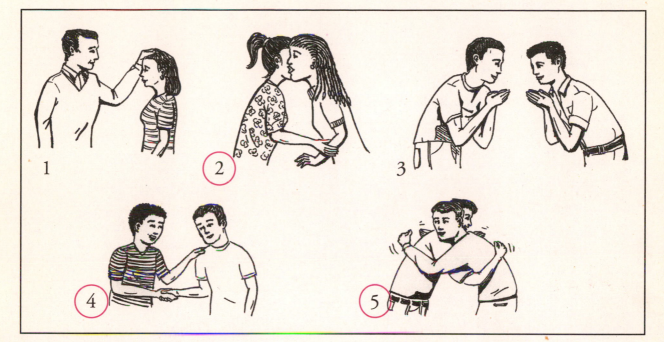

5 Puntuación

Rewrite the following sentences with the correct punctuation.

1. Hola! Cómo te llamas?
   ¡Hola! ¿Cómo te llamas?

2. Mucho gusto, Sonia!
   ¡Mucho gusto, Sonia!

3. ¿Cómo se escribe Javier? Con jota?
   ¿Cómo se escribe Javier? ¿Con jota?

4. Yo me llamo Antonio. ¿Y tú.
   Yo me llamo Antonio. ¿Y tú?

5. Hasta luego, Beatriz!
   ¡Hasta luego, Beatriz!

6. ¡Adiós, Ricardo.
   ¡Adiós, Ricardo!

6 América del Norte, América Central y el Caribe

Identify the Spanish-speaking countries in the following map. Write the name of each country in the space provided. You may refer to the maps in the textbook of Central America, Mexico and the Caribbean.

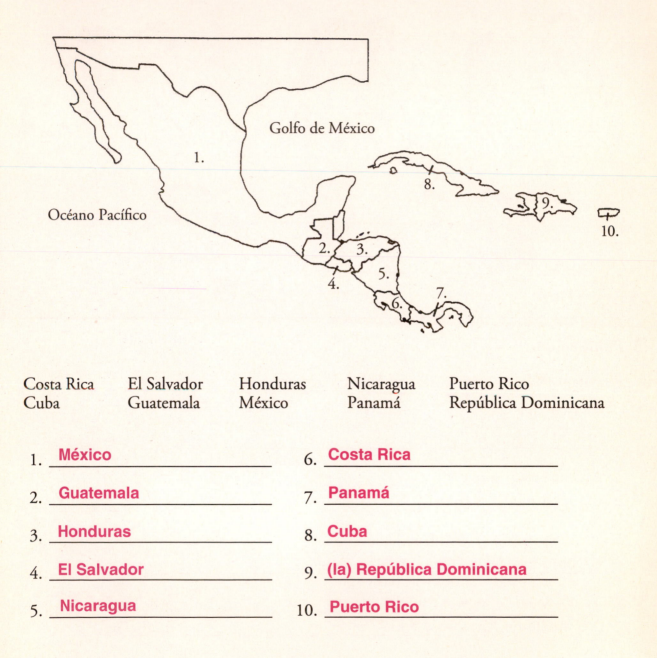

Costa Rica   El Salvador   Honduras   Nicaragua   Puerto Rico
Cuba   Guatemala   México   Panamá   República Dominicana

1. **México**

2. **Guatemala**

3. **Honduras**

4. **El Salvador**

5. **Nicaragua**

6. **Costa Rica**

7. **Panamá**

8. **Cuba**

9. **(la) República Dominicana**

10. **Puerto Rico**

EMC Español 1A

¡Aventura!

Workbook
Teacher's Edition

Karin D. Fajardo

EMC
Publishing

ST. PAUL • INDIANAPOLIS

Editorial Director
Alex Vargas

Associate Editor
Kimberly Rodrigues

Production Specialist
Julie Johnston

Cartoon Illustrator
Kristen M. Copham Kuelbs

The Internet is a fast-paced technology, and Web pages and Web addresses are constantly changing or disappearing. You may need to substitute different addresses from the ones given in the activities throughout this workbook.

ISBN 978-0-82196-228-2

Published by EMC/Paradigm Publishing
875 Montreal Way
St. Paul, Minnesota 55102
800-328-1452
www.emcschool.com
E-mail: educate@emcp.com

Printed in the United States of America
20 19 18 17 16 15 14 13 12 11   1 2 3 4 5 6 7 8 9 10

Capítulo 1

◈ Lección A

1 ¡Hola!

Unscramble the following conversation between two new students. Number each line 1–6 to show the correct order.

___1___   ¡Hola! ¿Cómo te llamas?

___7___   ¡Adiós, Natalia!

___3___   Yo me llamo Luis.

___5___   Se escribe con ele mayúscula, u, i, ese.

___6___   Hasta luego, Luis.

___4___   ¡Mucho gusto! ¿Cómo se escribe Luis?

___2___   Me llamo Natalia. ¿Y tú?

2 ¿Cómo se escribe?

Look at the following listing of the editorial staff of a Spanish-language magazine. Find the first name that corresponds to each clue and write it in the space provided.

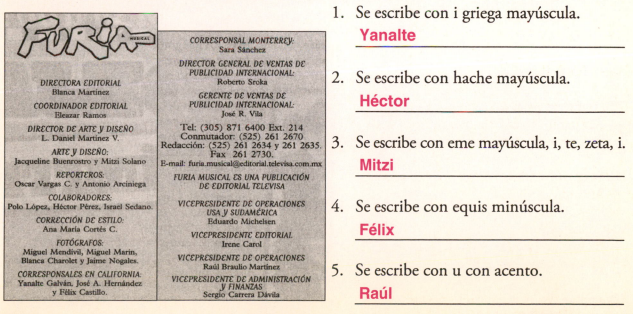

FURIA MUSICAL

DIRECTORA EDITORIAL
Blanca Martínez

COORDINADOR EDITORIAL
Eleazar Ramos

DIRECTOR DE ARTE Y DISEÑO
L. Daniel Martínez V.

ARTE Y DISEÑO:
Jacqueline Buenrostro y Mitzi Solano

REPORTEROS:
Oscar Vargas C. y Antonio Arciniega

COLABORADORES:
Polo López, Héctor Pérez, Israel Sedano.

CORRECCIÓN DE ESTILO:
Ana María Cortés C.

FOTÓGRAFOS:
Miguel Mendivil, Miguel Marín,
Blanca Charolet y Jaime Nogales.

CORRESPONSALES EN CALIFORNIA:
Yanalte Galván, José A. Hernández
y Félix Castillo.

CORRESPONSAL MONTERREY:
Sara Sánchez

DIRECTOR GENERAL DE VENTAS DE
PUBLICIDAD INTERNACIONAL:
Roberto Sroka

GERENTE DE VENTAS DE
PUBLICIDAD INTERNACIONAL:
José R. Vila

Tel: (305) 871 6400 Ext. 214
Conmutador: (525) 261 2670
Redacción: (525) 261 2634 y 261 2635.
Fax 261 2730.
E-mail: furia.musical@editorial.televisa.com.mx

FURIA MUSICAL ES UNA PUBLICACIÓN
DE EDITORIAL TELEVISA

VICEPRESIDENTE DE OPERACIONES
USA Y SUDAMÉRICA
Eduardo Michelsen

VICEPRESIDENTE EDITORIAL
Irene Carol

VICEPRESIDENTE DE OPERACIONES
Raúl Braulio Martínez

VICEPRESIDENTE DE ADMINISTRACIÓN
Y FINANZAS
Sergio Carrera Dávila

1. Se escribe con i griega mayúscula.
   Yanalte

2. Se escribe con hache mayúscula.
   Héctor

3. Se escribe con eme mayúscula, i, te, zeta, i.
   Mitzi

4. Se escribe con equis minúscula.
   Félix

5. Se escribe con u con acento.
   Raúl

3 Sopa de letras

In the word square find and circle ten Spanish names. The words may read vertically, horizontally or diagonally.

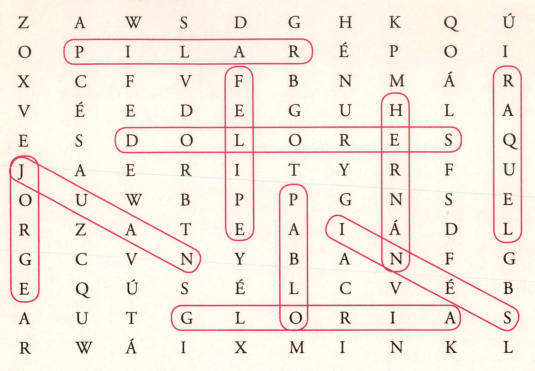

Z A W S D G H K Q Ú
O P I L A R É P O I
X C F V F B N M Á R
V É E D E G U H L A
E S D O L O R E S Q
J A E R I T Y R F U
O U W B P P G N S E
R Z A T E A I Á D L
G C V N Y B A N F G
E Q Ú S É L C V É B
A U T G L O R I A S
R W Á I X M I N K L

7 Europa, África y América del Sur

Write the names of the Spanish-speaking countries indicated by each number. Refer to the maps in the textbook of Europe, Africa and South America.

1. **Colombia**

2. **Venezuela**

3. **(el) Ecuador**

4. **(el) Perú**

5. **Bolivia**

6. **(el) Paraguay**

7. **Chile**

8. **(el) Uruguay**

9. **(la) Argentina**

10. **España**

11. **Guinea Ecuatorial**

8 Matemáticas

Write a number word in Spanish to answer each math problem.

MODELO   1 + 2 = <u>tres</u>

1. 2 + 3 = <u>cinco</u>
2. 4 + 5 = <u>nueve</u>
3. 9 − 2 = <u>siete</u>
4. 10 x 2 = <u>veinte</u>
5. 6 + 6 = <u>doce</u>

6. 8 x 2 = <u>dieciséis</u>
7. 19 − 9 = <u>diez</u>
8. 5 x 3 = <u>quince</u>
9. 12 − 4 = <u>ocho</u>
10. 10 + 4 = <u>catorce</u>

9 Más números

Following the pattern, write the next number word.

MODELO   cuatro, ocho, doce, <u>dieciséis</u>

1. dos, cuatro, seis, ocho, <u>diez</u>
2. cero, cinco, diez, quince, <u>veinte</u>
3. uno, cinco, nueve, trece, <u>diecisiete</u>
4. veinte, dieciocho, dieciséis, <u>catorce</u>
5. quince, catorce, trece, doce, <u>once</u>
6. tres, seis, nueve, doce, <u>quince</u>
7. doce, catorce, dieciséis, <u>dieciocho</u>
8. diecinueve, diecisiete, quince, <u>trece</u>

10 ¿Cuántos años tienes?

You have just asked the following students their ages. Write their responses, using the cues provided.

MODELO Ana / 13
Tengo trece años.

1. Roberto / 15
   Tengo quince años.

2. Marcos / 17
   Tengo diecisiete años.

3. Claudia / 14
   Tengo catorce años.

4. Elena / 16
   Tengo dieciséis años.

5. Diego / 12
   Tengo doce años.

6. Marta / 18
   Tengo dieciocho años.

11 ¿De dónde eres?

Imagine you are at a book convention where you ask several well-known Spanish-speaking writers where they are from. Following the model, write each response in the space provided.

MODELO Isabel Allende / Chile
Soy de Chile.

1. Julia Álvarez / República Dominicana
   Soy de (la) República Dominicana.

2. Carlos Fuentes / México
   Soy de México.

3. Gabriel García Márquez / Colombia
   Soy de Colombia.

4. Gary Soto / Estados Unidos
   Soy de (los) Estados Unidos.

5. Edgar Allan García / Ecuador
   Soy de(l) Ecuador.

6. Sandra Scoppettone / Argentina
   Soy de (la) Argentina.

7. Mario Vargas Llosa / Perú
   Soy de(l) Perú.

8. Esmeralda Santiago / Puerto Rico
   Soy de Puerto Rico.

12 Sí, soy de la capital

Match each question with the correct response.

1. __B__ ¿Eres del Perú?

2. __D__ ¿Eres de Nicaragua?

3. __A__ ¿Eres de Colombia?

4. __E__ ¿Eres de la República Dominicana?

5. __C__ ¿Eres de Chile?

A. Sí, soy de la capital, Bogotá.

B. Sí, soy de la capital, Lima.

C. Sí, soy de la capital, Santiago.

D. Sí, soy de la capital, Managua.

E. Sí, soy de la capital, Santo Domingo.

13 Soy de...

How would each person say where he or she is from? Following the model, write the response in the space provided. You might want to refer to the maps in the textbook.

MODELO   Soy de la Ciudad de México, la capital de México.

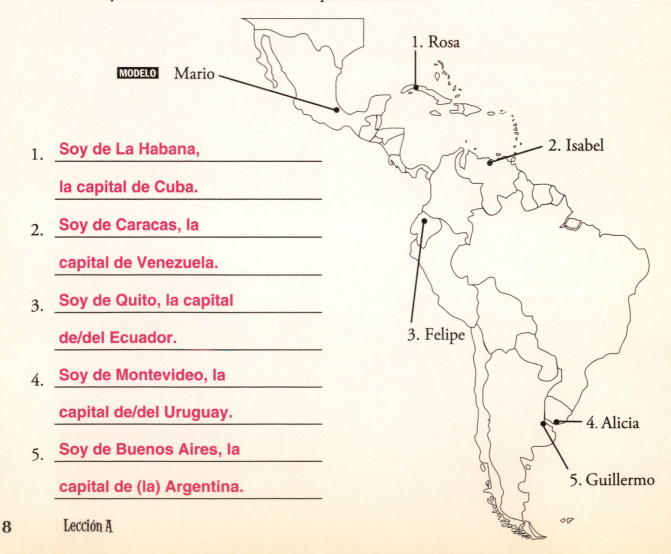

1. Soy de La Habana, la capital de Cuba.

2. Soy de Caracas, la capital de Venezuela.

3. Soy de Quito, la capital de/del Ecuador.

4. Soy de Montevideo, la capital de/del Uruguay.

5. Soy de Buenos Aires, la capital de (la) Argentina.

14 Los cognados

Look at the following Web site of a hotel. Find the Spanish words that are cognates to the list of English words below. Write each word in the corresponding space.

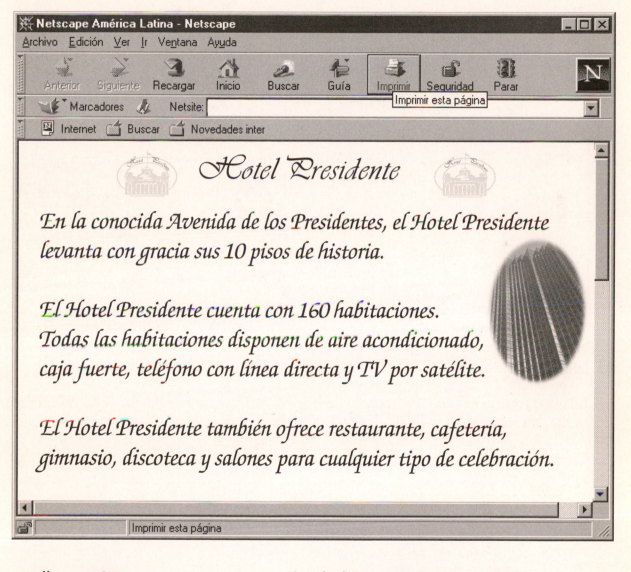

1. satellite **satélite**

2. president **presidente**

3. history **historia**

4. restaurant **restaurante**

5. celebration **celebración**

6. telephone **teléfono**

7. air **aire**

8. cafeteria **cafetería**

9. direct **directa**

10. discotheque **discoteca**

15 Oportunidades

Draw a circle around the professions where Spanish might be needed.

16 Diálogo completo

Imagine you are meeting Pedro, a Spanish-speaking student, for the first time. Write your side of the conversation in the spaces provided. Make sure the dialog follows a logical sequence.

PEDRO: ¡Hola!
TÚ: _____**¡Hola!**_____

PEDRO: ¿Cómo te llamas?
TÚ: _____**Me llamo (*student's name*). ¿Y tú?**_____

PEDRO: Yo me llamo Pedro.
TÚ: _____**Mucho gusto, Pedro.**_____

PEDRO: Mucho gusto. ¿De dónde eres?
TÚ: _____**Soy de (*answers will vary*). ¿Y tú? ¿Eres de aquí?**_____

PEDRO: No. Yo soy de El Salvador. ¿Cuántos años tienes?
TÚ: _____**Tengo (*student's age*). ¿Y tú?**_____

PEDRO: Yo tengo quince años.
TÚ: _____**Hasta luego.**_____

PEDRO: Adiós.

Lección B

1 ¿Qué tal?

Choose an appropriate response to each statement or question on the left.

__B__ 1. Buenas tardes.   A. Hasta mañana.   B. Buenas tardes, señora.

__A__ 2. ¿Qué tal?   A. Bien, gracias.   B. Me llamo Carmen.

__A__ 3. Bien, ¿y tú?   A. Estoy regular.   B. Buenas noches.

__B__ 4. ¿Cómo están?   A. Buenas tardes.   B. Mal, muy mal.

__A__ 5. Hasta mañana.   A. Hasta pronto.   B. Buenos días.

__B__ 6. Adiós.   A. ¡Hola!   B. Hasta luego.

__B__ 7. Buenas noches.   A. Bien, ¿y tú?   B. Hasta mañana.

2 Hasta mañana

Complete each sentence logically with the appropriate word.

1. Buenos __días__

2. __Buenas__ tardes.

3. ¿__Cómo__ están Uds.?

4. Estoy mal, muy __mal__.

5. ¿__Qué__ tal?

6. Bien, __gracias__

7. Buenas noches, __Señor(a)__ Torres.

8. __Hasta__ pronto, Juan.

9. ¿Cómo está __Ud.__, Sra. Chang?

10. __Buenas__ noches, Anita.

3 Saludos y despedidas

Look at the pictures below and think of what the people might be saying to each other. Write the expressions that best fit the situation inside the speech bubbles.

Answers will vary.

4 Los saludos en el mundo hispano

Circle the greetings that are appropriate for each time of the day.

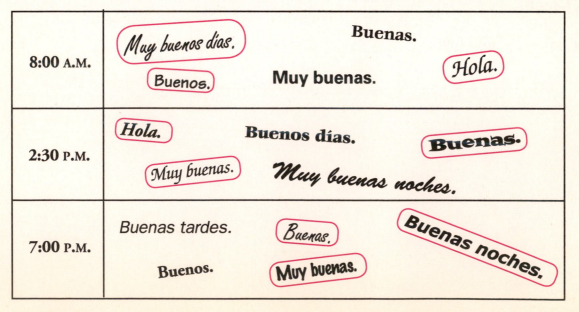

8:00 A.M.	*Muy buenos días.* Buenos.	Buenas. Muy buenas.	Hola.
2:30 P.M.	Hola. Muy buenas.	Buenos días. Muy buenas noches.	Buenas.
7:00 P.M.	Buenas tardes. Buenos.	Buenas. Muy buenas.	Buenas noches.

5 Saludos informales y formales

Are the following expressions appropriate to greet a friend or a person whom you would address with a title? Indicate which of the expressions are formal and which are informal. Write **F** for *formal* or **I** for *informal* in the space provided.

1. __F__ Muy buenos días.

2. __I__ ¿Qué tal?

3. __I__ ¿Cómo estás?

4. __I__ ¡Hola!

5. __F__ ¿Cómo está Ud.?

6. __F__ Buenas tardes.

6 Pronombres personales

How would you address the following people in Spanish? Write *tú, usted, ustedes, vosotros* or *vosotras* in the space provided.

1. Marta and Carlos, your friends from Mexico: __ustedes__

2. your little brother: __tú__

3. the parent of a classmate: __usted__

4. Victoria and Josefina, your friends from Spain: __vosotras__

5. the governor of your state: __usted__

6. Hugo and Armando, your friends from Spain: __vosotros__

7 Crucigrama

Complete the crossword puzzle with the correct spelling of the numbers provided.

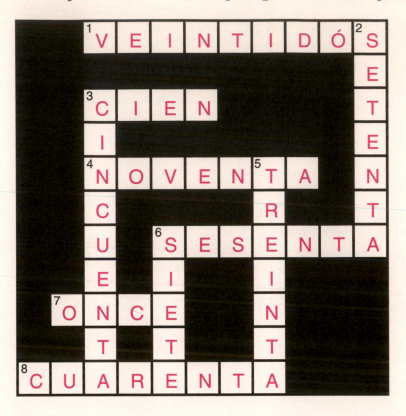

Horizontal	Vertical
1. 22	2. 70
3. 100	3. 50
4. 90	5. 30
6. 60	6. 7
7. 11	
8. 40	

Nombre: _____ Fecha: _____

8 Cheques personales

Complete the following checks by writing out each sum.

Bancomer   **CHEQUE NO. 6654**

PÁGUESE A LA
ORDEN DE ____I.N. E._____ $ ___55.00___

EN LETRAS LA
SUMA DE ____**cincuenta y cinco**_____ PESOS.

6654 7654 01001 007634521

Bancomer   **CHEQUE NO. 6655**

PÁGUESE A LA
ORDEN DE ____Joaquín Sandoval_____ $ ___26.00___

EN LETRAS LA
SUMA DE ____**veintiséis**_____ PESOS.

6654 7654 01001 007634521

Bancomer   **CHEQUE NO. 6656**

PÁGUESE A LA
ORDEN DE ____Novedades_____ $ ___87.00___

EN LETRAS LA
SUMA DE ____**ochenta y siete**_____ PESOS.

6654 7654 01001 007634521

---

9 Números de teléfono

Write the telephone number of each restaurant given, following the model.

MODELO Las Rejas: <u>dieciséis, diez, ochenta y nueve</u>

1. Mesón Casas Colgadas:
   veintidós, treinta y cinco, cincuenta y dos

2. Adolfo:
   treinta y dos, setenta y tres, quince

3. Gran Mesón:
   veintidós, setenta y dos, treinta y nueve

4. Amparito Rico:
   veintiuno, cuarenta y seis, treinta y nueve

5. Minaya:
   veintiuno, ochenta y dos, cincuenta y tres

6. Mesón de Pincelín:
   treinta y cuatro, sesenta, cero siete

10 Con cortesía

Look at the people in the drawing and imagine what they would say in each situation. Choose an appropriate expression from the word box and write it inside the speech bubble.

11 Las horas del día

Sort the following times of day from earliest to latest. Number each line 1–8 to show the correct order.

__5__ 1. Son las dos y media de la tarde.

__6__ 2. Son las nueve de la noche.

__3__ 3. Es mediodía.

__2__ 4. Son las nueve menos veinte de la mañana.

__4__ 5. Son las dos menos diez de la tarde.

__8__ 6. Es medianoche.

__7__ 7. Son las diez y cuarto de la noche.

__1__ 8. Son las siete y diez de la mañana.

12 ¿Qué hora es?

What time is it? Look at each clock and write the correct time in the space provided.

1. **Son las siete y veinticinco.** _____

2. **Son las cuatro y diez.** _____

3. **Son las cinco y media.** _____

4. **Son las dos menos cuarto.** _____

5. **Son las siete menos cinco.** _____

6. **Es la una y cuarto.** _____

13 La geografía y la hora

Did you know that when it is seven o'clock in the morning in California, it is already four o'clock in the afternoon in Spain? Look at the following map showing various time zones. Use the clocks at the bottom of the map to help you answer each question.

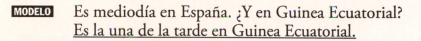

MODELO Es mediodía en España. ¿Y en Guinea Ecuatorial?
<u>Es la una de la tarde en Guinea Ecuatorial.</u>

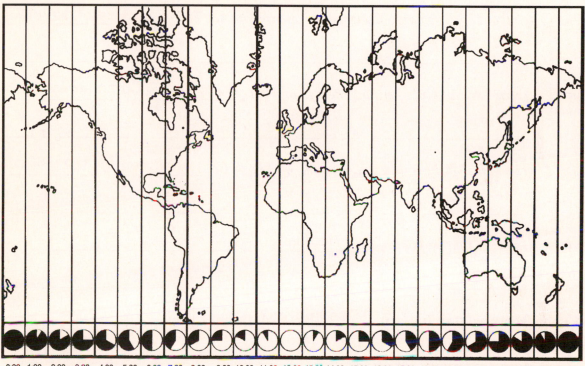

1. Es mediodía en España. ¿Y en Cuba?

   Son las siete de la mañana en Cuba.

2. Son las ocho de la mañana en México, D.F. ¿Y en Panamá?

   Son las diez de la mañana en Panamá.

3. Son las tres de la tarde en Chile. ¿Y en Guatemala?

   Son las dos de la tarde en Guatemala.

4. Son las seis de la noche en la República Dominicana. ¿Y en Nicaragua?

   Son las cinco de la tarde en Nicaragua.

5. Es medianoche en Colombia. ¿Y en España?

   Son las cinco de la mañana en España.

14 Diálogo completo

Use the cues provided to create a dialog between Sara y Sergio, two friends who bump into each other in the mall. **Possible answers:**

SERGIO: *(excuses himself as he bumps into someone)* (1) **Perdón.**

_____

SARA: *(calls out Sergio's name as she recognizes him and says hello)* (2) **¡Sergio! ¡Hola!**

_____

SERGIO: *(greets Sara and asks her how she is doing)* (3) **Hola, Sara. ¿Cómo estás?**

_____

SARA: *(responds that she is very well and asks how he is)* (4) **Muy bien. ¿Y tú?**

_____

SERGIO: *(responds that he is so-so)* (5) **Regular.**

_____

SARA: *(asks what time it is)* (6) **¿Qué hora es?**

_____

SERGIO: *(responds it is two fifteen in the afternoon)* (7) **Son las dos y cuarto**

de la tarde.

SARA: *(thanks him and politely lets him know she's about to walk away)* (8) **Gracias.**

Con permiso.

SERGIO: *(says see you later)* (9) **Hasta luego.**

SARA: *(says good-bye)* (10) **Adiós.**

Capítulo 2

Lección A

1 Preguntas y respuestas

Match each question on the left with the most logical response on the right.

__E__ 1. ¿Quién es él?   A. Isabel Gómez.

__A__ 2. ¿Cómo se llama ella?   B. Me llamo Rafael.

__F__ 3. ¿De dónde son ellos?   C. Él es de Chicago.

__B__ 4. ¿Quién eres tú?   D. No, ellas son de México.

__C__ 5. ¿De dónde es él?   E. Él es Juan.

__D__ 6. ¿Son las chicas de aquí? F. Ellos son de California.

2 ¿Quién es?

Diana and Alejo are at a party organized by the International Club. Complete the following conversation between them with the appropriate words.

ella   eres   llama   dónde   él   quién   es   soy   de

DIANA: Alejo, ¿(1) **quién** _____ es?

ALEJO: ¿Quién? ¿Ella?

DIANA: No, (2) **él** _____.

ALEJO: Se (3) **llama** _____ Ricardo.

DIANA: ¿De (4) **dónde** _____ es él?

ALEJO: Es (5) **de** _____ Venezuela.

DIANA: ¿Y (6) **ella** _____?

ALEJO: Laura (7) **es** _____ de Puerto Rico.

DIANA: ¿Y tú, Alejo? ¿De dónde (8) **eres** _____?

ALEJO: Yo (9) **soy** _____ de Nicaragua.

3 La influencia hispana en los Estados Unidos

Circle the words that have been borrowed from Spanish.

(chile) (patio) tennis university (rodeo) (adobe) encyclopedia

waffle chocolate umbrella circus (plaza) (mosquito) dinosaur

4 Geografía

Write the names of the states indicated by each number next to their English equivalent.

1. **Montana** _____ (Mountain)

2. **Nevada** _____ (Snow-covered)

3. **Colorado** _____ (Red-colored)

4. **Texas** _____ (Tiles)

5. **Florida** _____ (Flowered)

5 Pronombres personales

Rewrite the following sentences, replacing the underlined words with an appropriate subject pronoun.

MODELO   Joaquín y yo somos de Texas.
           Nosotros somos de Texas.

1. María González es de la Florida.

   Ella es de la Florida.

2. El señor y la señora López son de California.

   Ellos son de California.

3. Jorge es de la República Dominicana.

   Él es de la República Dominicana.

4. Magdalena y Pilar son de Arizona.

   Ellas son de Arizona.

5. Miguel y yo somos de los Estados Unidos.

   Nosotros somos de los Estados Unidos.

6. Marcos y Ronaldo son de Nueva York.

   Ellos son de Nueva York.

7. Me llamo Luisa. Olga y yo somos de Cuba.

   Me llamo Luisa. Nosotras somos de Cuba.

8. El Sr. Morales es de Puerto Rico.

   Él es de Puerto Rico.

9. La señora Núñez y la señorita Chávez son de El Paso.

   Ellas son de El Paso.

10. Tú y yo somos de aquí.

    Nosotros/as somos de aquí.

6 ¿De dónde son?

Write six sentences, telling where the following people are from.

MODELO   Alma es de Venezuela.

MODELO Alma

1. Cristina y Elvira
2. Andrés
3. tú
4. Sofía
5. nosotros
6. Miguel y Patricia

1. **Cristina y Elvira son de Colombia.**

2. **Andrés es de(l) Ecuador.**

3. **Tú eres de(l) Perú.**

4. **Sofía es de Bolivia.**

5. **Nosotros somos de Chile.**

6. **Miguel y Patricia son de (la) Argentina.**

Nombre: _____ Fecha: _____

7 No

Your friend is mistaken about the place of origin of the following famous people. Make the statements negative and then tell where they are from, using the cues provided.

MODELO Antonio Banderas es de México. (España)
Antonio Banderas no es de México. Es de España.

1. Celia Cruz es de Puerto Rico. (Cuba)

   Celia Cruz no es Puerto Rico. Es de Cuba.

2. Frida Kahlo y Diego Rivera son de Argentina. (México)

   Frida Kahlo y Diego Rivera no son de Argentina. Son de México.

3. Alex Rodríguez es de California. (Nueva York)

   Alex Rodríguez no es de California. Es de Nueva York.

4. Rigoberta Menchú es de Chile. (Guatemala)

   Rigoberta Menchú no es de Chile. Es de Guatemala.

5. Shakira y Juanes son de España. (Colombia)

   Shakira y Juanes no son de España. Son de Colombia.

8 A escribir

Use an item from each column to write five sentences.

yo	es	de México
Ud.	soy	de Nueva York
Juan y Ana	eres	de San Antonio
nosotros	son	de Puerto Rico
tú	somos	de los Estados Unidos

1. **Answers will vary.** _____

2. _____

3. _____

4. _____

5. _____

9 ¿Cómo se dice?

Match each question on the left with the correct response on the right.

__B__ 1. ¿Cómo se dice *backpack?*   A. Quiere decir *notebook.*

__F__ 2. ¿Cómo se dice *pencil?*   B. Se dice *mochila.*

__A__ 3. ¿Qué quiere decir *cuaderno?*   C. Se dice *ventana.*

__C__ 4. ¿Cómo se dice *window?*   D. Quiere decir *chair.*

__E__ 5. ¿Qué quiere decir *pizarra?*   E. Quiere decir *chalkboard.*

__D__ 6. ¿Qué quiere decir *silla?*   F. Se dice *lápiz.*

10 ¿Quién es?

Look at the drawing and read the questions. Write the name of the person in the space provided.

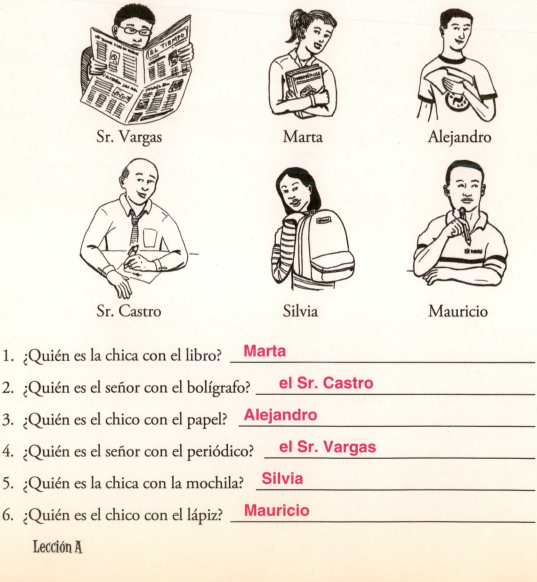

Sr. Vargas   Marta   Alejandro

Sr. Castro   Silvia   Mauricio

1. ¿Quién es la chica con el libro? __Marta__

2. ¿Quién es el señor con el bolígrafo? __el Sr. Castro__

3. ¿Quién es el chico con el papel? __Alejandro__

4. ¿Quién es el señor con el periódico? __el Sr. Vargas__

5. ¿Quién es la chica con la mochila? __Silvia__

6. ¿Quién es el chico con el lápiz? __Mauricio__

Crucigrama

11 Complete the following crossword puzzle with the Spanish words that correspond to the pictures.

Horizontal

1.

3.

5.

7.

9.

10.

Vertical

2.

4.

6.

7.

8.

12 Artículos definidos

Write *el, la, los* or *las* in the space provided.

> **MODELO**   el cuaderno

1. __el__ bolígrafo
2. __las__ amigas
3. __el__ profesor
4. __los__ libros

5. __el__ papel
6. __las__ mochilas
7. __el__ reloj
8. __los__ periódicos

9. __las__ paredes
10. __la__ silla
11. __las__ chicas
12. __el__ borrador

13 Identifica

Skim the following advertisement to identify five nouns. Write the nouns in the space provided and next to each one, write the letter **M** for masculine or **F** for feminine. Use the definite articles and the endings of the nouns as clues.

> **MODELO**   respuesta—F

RENAULT Scénic 2

Todo comenzó el día en que me compré el Scénic 2. Apenas me subí sentí el confort de un auto distinto. La posición de manejo sobreelevada, la gran visibilidad, la agilidad, la respuesta de su motor 2.0 L de 140 cv y la funcionalidad de todos sus comandos. Los asientos traseros individuales, el gran espacio interior y sobre todo la seguridad. Sentí que encontré otro espacio para mi vida, mi nueva vida. www.scenic2.com.ar

Salí, vivilo todo.

Possible answers:

1. __día—M; confort—M;__

2. __auto—M; posición—F;__

3. __visibilidad—F; agilidad—F;__

4. __motor—M; funcionalidad—F;__

5. __asientos—M; espacio—M; seguridad—F__

14 Plurales

Change the following words to the plural form.

MODELO   un libro ➔ <u>unos libros</u>

1. un papel   ➔ <u>**unos papeles**</u>

2. un lápiz   ➔ <u>**unos lápices**</u>

3. una mochila ➔ <u>**unas mochilas**</u>

4. una revista   ➔ <u>**unas revistas**</u>

5. un profesor ➔ <u>**unos profesores**</u>

6. una profesora ➔ <u>**unas profesoras**</u>

15 ¿Qué son?

Identify the illustrated objects, following the model.

MODELO   <u>Es una regla.</u>

1. <u>**Es un reloj.**</u>

2. <u>**Es un cuaderno.**</u>

3. <u>**Es un bolígrafo.**</u>

4. <u>**Son unos lápices.**</u>

5. <u>**Son unos libros.**</u>

16 ¿Qué hay en la clase?

For each item listed, say whether it is found in your classroom. If it is, include how many.
Follow the model.

> **MODELO**   mapa: <u>Hay dos mapas. / No hay un mapa.</u>

1. cesto de papeles: __**Answers will vary.**_____

2. estudiante: _____

3. puerta: _____

4. ventana: _____

5. silla: _____

6. pared: _____

7. sacapuntas: _____

8. reloj: _____

9. pizarra: _____

10. pupitre: _____

17 ¿Qué tienes en la mochila?

Make a list of the school supplies you carry in your backpack. Be sure to include the appropriate
indefinite articles.

En mi mochila tengo…

○   **Answers will vary.**

Lección B

1 ¿Qué clase es?

Match each class with its appropriate subject matter.

__F__ 1. matemáticas   A. la historia y la cultura de España

__A__ 2. español   B. los animales y las plantas

__B__ 3. biología   C. Picasso, Monet, Van Gogh

__C__ 4. arte   D. *Romeo y Julieta* de Shakespeare

__E__ 5. música   E. Bach, Mozart, Beethoven

__D__ 6. inglés   F. álgebra, geometría, trigonometría

2 Siete colores

In the word-square puzzle, find and circle seven names of colors. The words may read horizontally, vertically or diagonally.

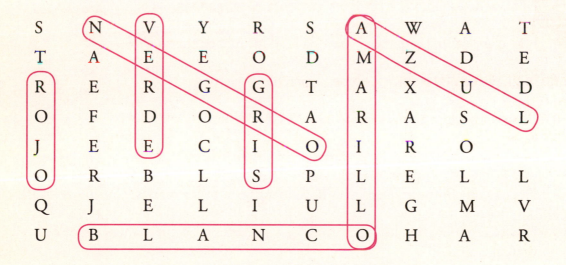

3 ¿Sí o no?

Read the statements and decide whether they are true or false, based on Elena's class schedule. If the statement is true, write *sí* in the space provided. If it is false, write *no*.

El horario de clases de Elena					
HORA	LUNES	MARTES	MIÉRCOLES	JUEVES	VIERNES
8:00 A.M.	matemáticas	matemáticas	matemáticas	matemáticas	matemáticas
8:50 A.M.	español	español	español	español	español
10:40 A.M.	historia	historia	historia	historia	historia
11:45 A.M.	inglés	computación	inglés	computación	inglés
12:35 A.M.	almuerzo	almuerzo	almuerzo	almuerzo	almuerzo
1:45 P.M.	biología	biología	biología	biología	biología
2:35 P.M.	arte	música	arte	música	arte

__sí__ 1. Elena tiene seis clases en un día.

__sí__ 2. La clase de matemáticas es a las ocho de la mañana.

__no__ 3. La clase de español es a las diez y cuarenta de la mañana.

__no__ 4. Hay clase de inglés martes y jueves a las doce menos cuarto.

__sí__ 5. No hay clase de música los lunes, miércoles y viernes.

__no__ 6. El almuerzo es a la una y cuarenta y cinco de la tarde.

__sí__ 7. Elena tiene clase de biología a las dos menos cuarto.

__sí__ 8. La clase de computación es a las doce menos cuarto los martes y los jueves.

__no__ 9. Hay clase de historia los lunes, miércoles y viernes a las nueve menos diez de la mañana.

__no__ 10. Las clases de Elena terminan a la una y treinta y cinco de la tarde.

4 Los colegios en el mundo hispano

Read the following statements. Based on what you have learned about schools in Spain, decide whether they refer to a typical high school in the United States or in Spain. Write **U.S.** or **Spain** in the space provided.

U.S. _____ 1. Students actively participate in class.

U.S. _____ 2. Schools offer many extracurricular activities.

Spain _____ 3. All students follow the same demanding curriculum.

Spain _____ 4. Courses are taught through lectures.

U.S. _____ 5. Quizzes and exams are common throughout the year.

Spain _____ 6. A comprehensive exam at the end of the year determines whether a student passes or fails.

5 Sustantivos y adjetivos

For each sentence, underline the noun and circle the adjective. Then, check the appropriate columns to indicate whether it is masculine or feminine and singular or plural. Follow the model.

	Masculine	Feminine	Singular	Plural
MODELO Daniel lleva una camiseta (nueva.)		√	√	
1. Sergio es un estudiante (nuevo.)	√		√	
2. La chica (nueva) es de México.		√	√	
3. Los zapatos son (negros.)	√			√
4. Las paredes son (blancas.)		√		√
5. Ella lleva una blusa (amarilla.)		√	√	
6. Necesito unos lápices (rojos.)	√			√

6 La ropa y los colores

Maricela is talking on her cell phone, describing what people are wearing to the party. Complete her statements with the correct form of the adjective in parenthesis. Be sure the adjective agrees in gender and number with the noun it describes.

MODELO Arturo lleva una camiseta roja. (rojo)

1. Nuria y Pilar llevan unas blusas **blancas** _____. (blanco)

2. Mi amigo Pepe lleva unos calcetines **rojos** _____. (rojo)

3. Mabel lleva una falda **amarilla** _____. (amarillo)

4. Mauricio lleva unos zapatos **grises** _____. (gris)

5. Dos chicos llevan unos jeans **negros** _____. (negro)

6. Los pantalones de Selena son **verdes** _____. (verde)

7. Yo llevo pantalones **azules** _____. Son **nuevos** _____. (azul, nuevo)

7 En el colegio

Complete each sentence logically with the appropriate verb form. You will need to use one verb twice.

hablar   llevar   necesitar   terminar   estudiar

MODELO La señora Sánchez habla inglés y español.

1. Jaime y yo **necesitamos** _____ papel para la clase de arte.

2. Los estudiantes **llevan** _____ pantalones grises y camisas blancas.

3. La clase de historia **termina** _____ al mediodía.

4. ¿**Estudias** _____ tú computación?

5. Yo **estudio** _____ en el Colegio Cervantes.

6. Gabriela **habla** _____ español muy bien.

8 ¿Qué necesitan?

Write a sentence telling what the person(s) need(s). Use the pictures as clues and the correct forms of the verb *necesitar* and the adjective *nuevo*. Follow the model.

MODELO  Sara

Sara necesita un lápiz nuevo.

1.  nosotros

   Nosotros necesitamos zapatos nuevos.

2.  Pedro

   Pedro necesita una regla nueva.

3.  Ana y Lupe

   Ana y Lupe necesitan mochilas nuevas.

4.  yo

   Yo necesito un reloj nuevo.

5. Ernesto

   Ernesto necesita un pupitre nuevo.

6. tú

   Tú necesitas una camiseta nueva.

9 Radio Nacional

Answer the questions based on the following schedule for an Argentinian radio station. Note that in Argentina, the 24-hour clock is used. In this system, 14.00 is the same as two o'clock in the afternoon.

MODELO   ¿A qué hora es "De Segovia a…"?
Es a las nueve de la noche.

FM Música

Radio Nacional

6.00:	La mañana de Radio Nacional.
9.00:	El órgano (A. Gómez).
10.00:	Cuadro de situación (S. Crivelli).
11.00:	Aproximación a la ópera (Juan Carlos Montero).
13.00:	Bailando sobre el Titanic.
14.00:	Intimidad con la música.
16.00:	Teatro Cervantes.
16.30:	Operamante (C. Ratier).
20.00:	Discoteca F. M. 96.7
21.00:	De Segovia a... con S. Domínguez.
22.00:	España y su música (O. Monzo).
23.00:	Discoteca.
24.00:	Clásicos Siglo XX, con Alicia Terzián.

1. ¿A qué hora es "El órgano"?

   Es a las nueve de la mañana.

2. ¿A qué hora es "Bailando sobre el Titanic"?

   Es a la una de la tarde.

3. ¿A qué hora termina el Teatro Cervantes?

   Termina a las cuatro y media de la tarde.

4. ¿A qué hora es "España y su música"?

   Es a las diez de la noche.

5. ¿Qué hay a las once de la noche?

   Hay "Discoteca".

6. ¿A qué hora es "Clásicos Siglo XX"?

   Es a la medianoche.

10 La computadora

Identify the parts of the computer in the following illustration.

1. __la pantalla__

4. __la impresora láser__

2. __los diskettes__

3. __el teclado__

5. __el ratón__

6. __los discos compactos__

11 Números y direcciones

Your friend is interested in staying at Hotel San Roque, a small hotel in Spain. Use the information in this magazine clipping to answer his questions.

A. DIRECCIÓN: Esteban de Ponte, 32. 38450, Garachico. Tenerife. Tel.: 922 13 34 35. Fax: 922 13 34 06. Web: www.hotelsanroque.com E-mail: info@hotelsanroque.com **B. ACCESOS:** autopista T1 hasta el Puerto de la Cruz. De ahí, tomar la C-820 hasta Icod de los Vinos y Garachico. En el mismo Garachico, seguir indicaciones hasta el hotel, que está a unos 25 kilometros del Puerto de la Cruz. **C. CATEGORÍA:** tres estrellas. **D. INSTALACIONES:** nueve habitaciones dobles, siete dúplex, dos *junior suites* y dos *suites* con baño completo, caja fuerte, minibar, TV, video y equipo de música, sala de lectura y salón social, patio-bar, sauna, solario y piscina climatizada. **E. GASTRONOMÍA:** cocina de mercado, asesorada por el restaurante Celler de Can Roca en Girona. **F. PRECIOS:** doble estándar: 175 €; dúplex: 187 €; *junior suite:* 225 €; *suite:* 247 €. Desayuno incluido.

1. ¿Cuál es el número de teléfono? __922 13 34 35__

2. ¿Cuál es la dirección de correo electrónico? __info@hotelsanroque.com__

3. ¿Cuál es la dirección de Internet? __www.hotelsanroque.com__

4. ¿Cuál es el número de fax? __922 13 34 06__

12 Las notas

Use the grading scale to convert the following grades for your Mexican pen pal. Write S, EX, MB, B, NM or D in the space provided.

__EX__ 1. 90% en matemáticas

__B__ 2. 60% en historia

__S__ 3. 100% en arte

__D__ 4. 40% en música

__MB__ 5. 80% en español

__NM__ 6. 50% en biología

Escala	
10	Superior (S)
9	Excelente (EX)
8	Muy Bueno (MB)
7–6	Bueno (B)
5	Necesita Mejorar (NM)
4–0	Deficiente (D)

13 El verbo *estar*

Complete the following e-mail message with the correct forms of the verb *estar*.

	Normal	MIME	QP	Enviar

Para: Alicia
De: José
Asunto: Número de teléfono de Lorenzo
Cc:

¡Hola! ¿Cómo (1)__estás__ tú? Yo (2)__estoy__

muy bien. Carlos y yo (3)__estamos__ en Puerto Vallarta.

Puerto Vallarta (4)__está__ en México. Gabi y Paulina

(5)__están__ en la capital. No sé dónde

(6)__está__ mi cuaderno con los números de teléfono.

¿Tienes el número de teléfono de Lorenzo? Necesito hablar con él. ¡Gracias!

14 ¿Dónde está?

Look at the illustration of José's bedroom and answer the questions that follow.

MODELO   ¿Dónde está el reloj?
         <u>El reloj está en la pared.</u>

1. ¿Dónde está la computadora?
   Está en el escritorlo.
   _____

2. ¿Dónde está la mochila?
   Está sobre la silla.
   _____

3. ¿Dónde está el mapa de los Estados Unidos?
   Está en la pared.
   _____

4. ¿Dónde están los libros?
   Están en la mochila.
   _____

5. ¿Dónde están los papeles?
   Están en el cesto de papeles.
   _____

6. ¿Dónde está el disco compacto?
   Está sobre el teclado.
   _____

15 Diálogo completo

The school newspaper is going to write an article about a school in Mexico, but the reporter only recorded the answers of the student he interviewed. As the editor, write logical questions in the spaces provided. **Possible answers:**

1. **¿Cómo te llamas?** _____

   Me llamo Juan Carlos Macedo Olivas.

2. **¿Cuál es tu dirección de correo electrónico?** _____

   Mi correo electrónico es JCOlivas@telecom.mex.

3. **¿Cuál es tu número de teléfono?** _____

   Es el 9-76-13-32.

4. **¿Cómo se llama tu colegio?** _____

   Mi colegio se llama Preparatoria Nevada.

5. **¿Dónde está tu colegio?** _____

   Está en Guadalajara, México.

6. **¿Cuántas clases tienes en un día?** _____

   Tengo siete clases en un día.

7. **¿A qué hora terminan las clases?** _____

   Terminan a las tres de la tarde.

8. **¿Hay un examen mañana?** _____

   Sí, mañana hay un examen de historia.

9. **¿A qué hora es el examen?** _____

   El examen es a las diez y media de la mañana.

10. **¿Dónde está mi lápiz?** _____

    Allí está. Sobre la mesa.

Capítulo 3

Lección A

1 ¿Dónde están?

Where is everyone? Match the phrases in English on the left with the appropriate phrase in Spanish on the right. Write the letter of your choice in the space provided.

___C___ 1. Jorge is depositing a check.   A. Está en el cine.

___E___ 2. Margarita is getting her teeth cleaned.   B. Está en el parque.

___H___ 3. Laura is checking out a book.   C. Está en el banco.

___A___ 4. Gustavo is watching a movie.   D. Está en el médico.

___B___ 5. Guillermo is jogging.   E. Está en el dentista.

___G___ 6. Sr. López is teaching biology.   F. Está en el hotel.

___F___ 7. Sra. Sainz is resting after a long trip.   G. Está en la escuela.

___D___ 8. Josefina is getting a flu shot.   H. Está en la biblioteca.

2 ¡Vamos!

Roberto and Marta are at the park when Rocío shows up. Complete the conversation between them with the appropriate words.

encantada	quiero	simpática	vamos	mañana
por qué	presento	mucho gusto	cuándo	fiesta

MARTA: Allí está mi amiga Rocío. Es una chica (1)**simpática**_____. ¡Hola, Rocío!

ROCÍO: ¡Hola!

MARTA: Rocío, te (2)**presento**_____ a Roberto.

ROBERTO: (3)**Mucho gusto**_____.

ROCÍO: (4)**Encantada**_____. Saben, hay una (5)**fiesta**_____
          en la escuela. ¿(6)**Por qué**_____ no vamos?

MARTA: ¿(7)**Cuándo**_____ es?

ROCÍO: Es (8)**mañana**_____ a las siete de la noche.

ROBERTO: Yo (9)**quiero**_____ ir.

MARTA: ¡(10)**Vamos**_____!

Nombre: _____ Fecha: _____

3 De visita en la Ciudad de México

What places could you visit in Mexico City? Match the name of the place in Spanish on the left with the appropriate description in English on the right. Write the correct letter in the space provided.

__C__ 1. el Zócalo   A. the main temple of the ancient Aztec capital

__E__ 2. el Museo Nacional de Antropología   B. amusement park rides

__A__ 3. el Templo Mayor   C. the main plaza in the center of the city

__D__ 4. el Paseo de la Reforma   D. a wide street built by emperor Maximilian

__F__ 5. Chapultepec   E. exhibits of pre-Columbian cultures

__B__ 6. las atracciones   F. a very large park

4 En la fiesta

At a party, how would you introduce the guests? Complete the following introductions logically with the words *te*, *le* or *les*.

MODELO   Eugenio, <u>te</u> presento a mi amiga Anabel.

1. Sr. y Sra. Ortega, **les** presento a la profesora de arte.

2. Arturo, **te** presento a Sergio, el amigo de Alma.

3. Profesora Prieto, **le** presento a Vero y Carla.

4. Blanca y Ángela, **les** presento a Hugo y Raúl.

5. Miguel, **te** presento al señor Gómez, mi profesor de español.

6. Don Rodrigo, **le** presento a mi amiga Lupe.

7. Vero y Carla, **les** presento a doña Violeta.

8. Señor Gómez, **le** presento a Sergio y Alma.

9. Gabi, **te** presento al amigo de doña Violeta.

10. Hugo y Raúl, **les** presento a don Rodrigo.

5 Más presentaciones

Combine elements from each column to write five introductions. Be sure to use contractions when necessary.

MODELO   Clara, te presento al señor Portillo.

Clara	te presento a	mis amigos Diego y Tomás
Srta. Guzmán	le presento a	el profesor de computación
Enrique	les presento a	el señor Portillo
don Humberto		doña Esperanza
Sr. y Sra. Ramírez		el estudiante de Honduras
Daniel y Nicolás		el amigo de Fernando

Possible answers:

1. Srta. Guzmán, le presento al amigo de Fernando.

2. Enrique, te presento al profesor de computación.

3. Don Humberto, le presento a mis amigos Diego y Tomás.

4. Sr. y Sra. Ramírez, les presento al estudiante de Honduras.

5. Daniel y Nicolás, les presento a doña Esperanza.

6 Mucho gusto

In the following drawing, Silvia is introducing José to the math teacher, Sr. Torres. Complete the speech bubbles with appropriate expressions.

7 Preguntas

Complete the following questions with the appropriate question words.

1. ¿**Cómo** te llamas?

2. ¿**Cuál** es tu dirección de correo electrónico?

3. ¿**Qué** quiere decir la palabra *escuela*?

4. ¿**Quiénes/Cuándo** van al restaurante?

5. ¿**Cuándo/Dónde** es la fiesta de Yolanda?

6. ¿**Dónde** están mis libros de inglés?

7. ¿**Por qué** no vamos al cine mañana?

8. ¿**Cuántos** escritorios hay en la oficina?

8 Más preguntas

Unscramble the words and write complete, logical questions.

MODELO ¿? / en / el parque / Sofía / camina
¿Camina Sofía en el parque?

1. ¿? / el amigo / simpático / de / verdad / Beatriz / es
   El amigo de Beatriz es simpático, ¿verdad?

2. ¿? / Andrés / Jaime / van / a / y / la fiesta
   ¿Van Andrés y Jaime a la fiesta?

3. ¿? / sabe / la fiesta / Julia / cuándo / es
   ¿Sabe Julia cuándo es la fiesta?

4. ¿? / es / mañana / no / la fiesta
   La fiesta es mañana, ¿no?

5. ¿? / Uds. / la biblioteca / van / a
   ¿Van Uds. a la biblioteca?

6. ¿? / las dos / la clase / termina / a
   ¿Termina la clase a las dos?

9 Viaje a Machu Picchu

A travel agency called Atalaya Turismo is planning a trip *(un viaje)* to the ruins of Machu Picchu in Peru. Look at the advertisement and write questions about the trip. Use the answers provided to help you write logical questions for each answer.

1. **¿Cuándo es el viaje?**
   _____

   El viaje *(trip)* es el 29 de noviembre.

2. **¿De cuántos días es el viaje?**
   _____

   El viaje es de siete días.

3. **¿Cómo se llama el hotel?**
   _____

   El hotel se llama Machu Picchu Inn.

4. **¿Cómo van a Machu Picchu?**
   _____

   Van en tren panorámico.

5. **¿Van a Arequipa?**
   _____

   No, no van a Arequipa.

6. **¿Cuál es el número de teléfono de Atalaya Turismo?**
   _____

   El número de teléfono de Atalaya Turismo es el 4312-5784.

Nombre: _____ Fecha: _____

10 Sopa de letras

In the word-square find and circle ten modes of transportation in Spanish. The words may read vertically, horizontally or diagonally.

W	E	C	A	M	I	Ó	N	E	R	T	Ó
T	Á	L	A	U	M	V	T	U	Z	L	S
B	P	B	A	R	C	O	Y	R	I	X	L
N	Z	I	Y	F	R	M	A	Ó	E	B	M
T	T	C	A	U	T	O	B	Ú	S	N	U
Í	D	I	F	V	U	T	D	O	O	P	L
V	S	C	Y	B	I	O	A	M	M	O	J
Q	Ú	L	Á	N	N	Ó	W	X	A	K	L
U	C	E	T	G	H	E	N	E	I	O	N
M	E	T	R	O	R	M	W	Y	U	I	D
R	S	A	N	S	P	Ó	R	T	A	B	É

11 ¿Cómo vamos?

How would you travel from one place to another? Write a mode of transportation that would make sense. In most cases, there is more than one possible answer.

MODELO   ¿De México, D.F. a Jalisco? en autobús **Possible answers:**

1. ¿De Chicago a México, D.F.? **en avión**

2. ¿De Cancún a Cozumel? **en barco**

3. ¿De México, D.F. a Puebla? **en carro**

4. ¿Del Zócalo a Chapultepec? **en metro**

5. ¿De la escuela al cine? **en autobús**

6. ¿Del hotel a un restaurante cerca? **a pie**

12 Un mensaje electrónico

Complete the following e-mail with the correct forms of the verb *ir*.

| ▼ | Normal ▼ | MIME ▼ | QP 🗐 🗐 •| 🗐 | **Enviar** |

Para: Irene
De: Natalia
Asunto: Fiesta
Cc:

¡Hola, Irene!

Sabes, Félix y yo no (1) **vamos** _____ a la fiesta mañana. Félix no

(2) **va** _____ porque él y un amigo (3) **van** _____ al

cine. Yo no (4) **voy** _____ porque no tengo transporte y la fiesta

está lejos. Iván tampoco (5) **va** _____ porque

(6) **va** _____ al dentista. Rebeca y Antonio sí

(7) **van** _____ . ¿Y tú? ¿(8) **Vas** _____ a la fiesta?

¿Cómo (9) **vas** _____ tú? ¿Tienes transporte?

¿(10) **Vamos** _____ tú y yo juntas *(together)*?

Hasta luego,

Natalia

13 ¿Quiénes van?

Complete the sentences with the appropriate subjects from the list.

yo   tú   vosotras   mis amigos   Leonardo   nosotros

1. **Mis amigos** _____ van a la escuela a pie.

2. **Vosotras** _____ vais al cine, ¿verdad?

3. **Leonardo** _____ no va a la biblioteca con Manuel.

4. **Yo** _____ voy al banco en taxi.

5. **Nosotros** _____ no vamos a la fiesta de Raquel.

6. **Tú** _____ vas a la oficina a las ocho, ¿verdad?

14 ¿Cómo van?

Write complete sentences saying how the following people get to their workplaces.

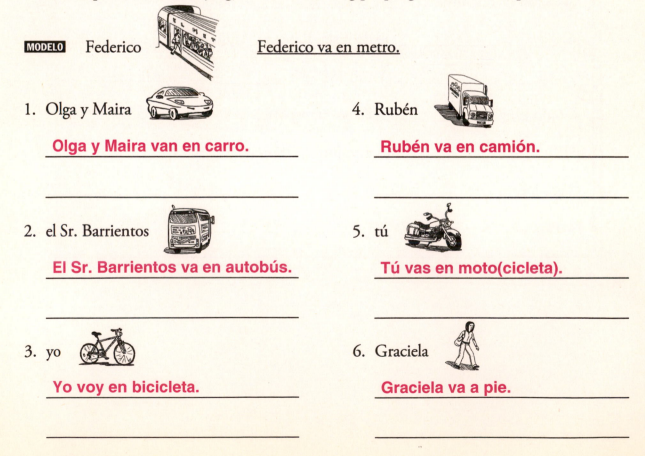

MODELO   Federico   Federico va en metro.

1. Olga y Maira

   Olga y Maira van en carro.

2. el Sr. Barrientos

   El Sr. Barrientos va en autobús.

3. yo

   Yo voy en bicicleta.

4. Rubén

   Rubén va en camión.

5. tú

   Tú vas en moto(cicleta).

6. Graciela

   Graciela va a pie.

15 ¿Adónde y a qué hora van?

Combine elements from each column to write six complete sentences. Add any necessary words and make changes as needed.

MODELO <u>Eduardo va a la médica a las dos de la tarde.</u>

Eduardo	escuela	8:15 A.M.
mis amigos	cine	10:00 A.M.
tú	banco	12:00 P.M.
el estudiante nuevo	fiesta	2:00 P.M.
don Ignacio	parque	4:30 P.M.
Alicia y Gloria	médica	6:45 P.M.
Juan y yo	biblioteca	7:30 P.M.
la profesora	restaurante	8:45 P.M.

1. **Answers will vary.** _____

_____

2. _____

_____

3. _____

_____

4. _____

_____

5. _____

_____

6. _____

_____

16 Playa del Carmen

Some of your friends are thinking of going to Playa del Carmen, a popular beach in Mexico. They would like more information about the place: how to get there, is it close to Cancún, a name of a fantastic hotel, what is in Xcaret, etc. Prepare a list of six to eight questions in Spanish to ask a local Mexican travel agency. If you would like, search the Internet for the answers to your questions.

Possible answers: ¿Cómo vamos a Playa del Carmen? ¿Está cerca de Cancún? ¿Está Tulum lejos? ¿Vamos en autobús a Tulum? ¿Cómo se llama un hotel fantástico? ¿Hay un cine en Playa del Carmen? ¿Cuántos restaurantes hay? ¿Son los muchachos simpáticos? ¿Hablan inglés? ¿Tomamos un barco a Cozumel? ¿Qué hay en Xcaret? ¿A qué hora vamos a Xcaret?

◈ Lección B

1 Crucigrama

Complete the following crossword puzzle with words related to downtown.

Horizontal

5. La oficina está en un _____ grande.

6. Hay muchos edificios en el _____.

7. El concierto de rock va a ser en la _____.

8. Una _____ es una calle grande.

Vertical

1. Vamos al _____ de arte.

2. El actor está en el _____.

3. La _____ de México es grande.

4. Voy a la _____ porque necesito ropa nueva.

6. Los carros van por la _____.

2 En el Distrito Federal

Imagine you took the following photographs during a trip to Mexico City. Identify what is shown in each photograph.

MODELO

Es un museo.

1.   **Possible answers:**

Es una plaza.

_____

2.

Es un edificio grande.

_____

3.

Es un teatro.

_____

4.

Es una avenida.

_____

5.

Es un restaurante.

_____

6.

Es una tienda.

_____

3 ¿Adónde van a ir?

Look at the map of the center of Mexico City. Write complete sentences, telling where each person is going to go.

MODELO   Yo voy a ir al Zócalo.

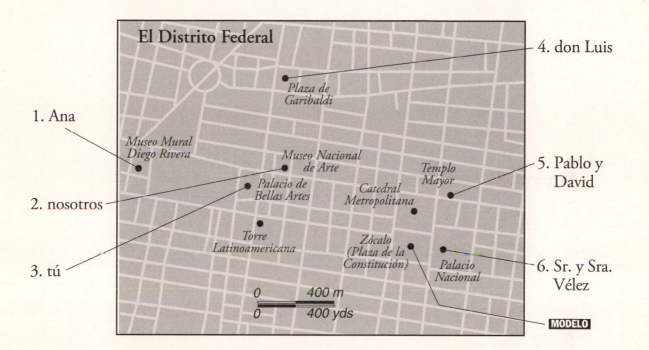

El Distrito Federal

4. don Luis

Plaza de Garibaldi

1. Ana

Museo Mural Diego Rivera

Museo Nacional de Arte

5. Pablo y David

Templo Mayor

2. nosotros

Palacio de Bellas Artes

Catedral Metropolitana

Torre Latinoamericana

3. tú

Zócalo (Plaza de la Constitución)

Palacio Nacional

6. Sr. y Sra. Vélez

0   400 m
0   400 yds

MODELO

1. **Ana va a ir al Museo Mural Diego Rivera.**

2. **Nosotros vamos a ir al Museo Nacional de Arte.**

3. **Tú vas a ir al Palacio de Bellas Artes.**

4. **Don Luis va a ir a la Plaza de Garibaldi.**

5. **Pablo y David van a ir al Templo Mayor.**

6. **Sr. y Sra. Vélez van a ir al Palacio Nacional.**

4 ¿Qué van a hacer?

Look at the illustrations and write complete sentences, telling what the people are going to do. Use the construction *ir + a* and the verbs from the list.

estudiar	tomar	necesitar
hablar	ir	caminar

MODELO Ángela
Ángela va a ir al museo.

1. Rafael

   Rafael va a hablar por teléfono.

2. los señores

   Los señores van a tomar el tren.

3. Diana

   Diana va a estudiar.

4. nosotros

   Nosotros vamos a ir al cine.

5. Gustavo

   Gustavo va a caminar.

6. yo

   Yo voy a necesitar una

   silla nueva.

5 En el restaurante

Complete the following conversation that takes place at a restaurant with the appropriate words from the box.

agua	para	menú	**ensalada**	comer	**momento**
tomar	cómo	**acuerdo**	jugo	veo	**siempre**

MESERO: Buenas tardes, señoritas. ¿Qué van a (1) **tomar** ?

JULIA: Hoy voy a tomar un (2) **jugo** de naranja.

CARMEN: Yo quiero un (3) **agua** mineral.

MESERO: ¡(4) **Cómo** no! ¿Y (5) **para** comer?

JULIA: Pues, quiero pescado pero no (6) **veo** pescado en el

(7) **menú** … ¡Aquí está! Yo quiero pescado con una

(8) **ensalada** .

MESERO: ¿Y Ud., señorita?

CARMEN: (9) **Siempre** como pollo pero hoy voy a

(10) **comer** pescado.

MESERO: De (11) **acuerdo** . Un

(12) **momento** , por favor.

6 Completa el menú

Imagine you work at Restaurante Los Amigos. Complete the menu by writing the items in the box under the appropriate headings.

naranja   refrescos   ensalada de tomate   pollo   frijoles

Restaurante Los Amigos

ENSALADAS

(1) **Ensalada de tomate** $3.50
Ensalada mixta $4.50

PLATOS TÍPICOS
Quesadillas.. $5.00
Tacos mixtos.. $6.25

(2) **Pollo** en mole.................................. $7.50
Enchiladas verdes.. $6.75

PLATOS VEGETARIANOS

(3) **Frijoles** negros......................... $4.50
Burritos vegeterianos.. $5.50

BEBIDAS

Jugo de (4) **naranja** $1.25

(5) **Refresco** $1.25
Agua mineral $1.25

7 ¿Quién comprende?

Tell who understands by completing each sentence with the present tense of *comprender*.

1. Nuria y yo **comprendemos**

2. Los estudiantes **comprenden**

3. La profesora Díaz **comprende**

4. Tú **comprendes**

5. Yo **comprendo**

6. Vosotros **comprendéis**

8 ¿Qué comen?

Write a sentence telling what each person eats.

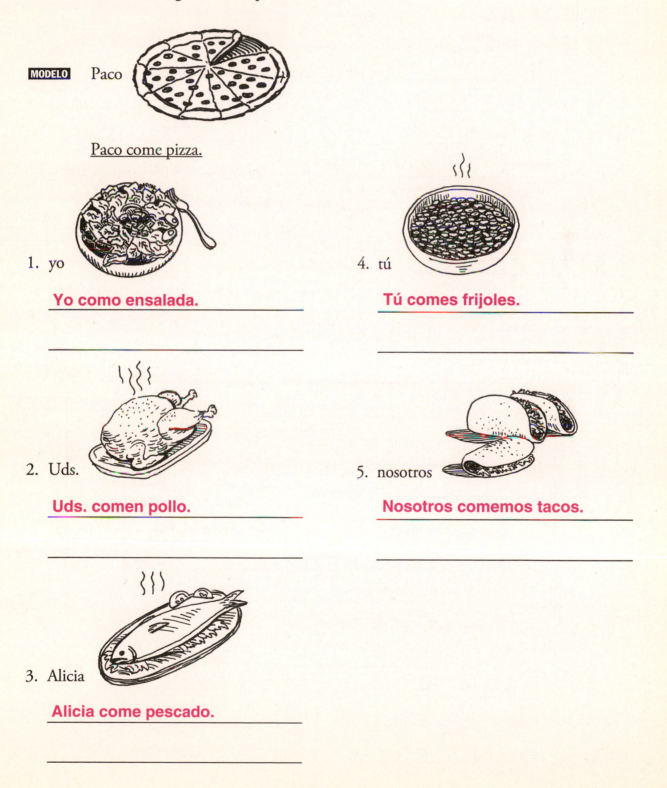

MODELO   Paco

Paco come pizza.

1. yo

Yo como ensalada.

4. tú

Tú comes frijoles.

2. Uds.

Uds. comen pollo.

5. nosotros

Nosotros comemos tacos.

3. Alicia

Alicia come pescado.

9 ¿Qué hacen?

What is everyone doing downtown? Complete the sentences with the present tense of the verbs in parentheses.

1. Carlos y Elvira **comen** _____ en el Restaurante Delicias. (comer)

2. Yo **veo** _____ el arte de Frida Kahlo en un museo. (ver)

3. Humberto **lee** _____ el periódico en la Plaza San Juan. (leer)

4. El médico le **hace** _____ una pregunta al señor Durán. (hacer)

5. Tú no **sabes** _____ dónde está la Plaza de la Constitución. (saber)

6. Nosotros **vemos** _____ muchos museos y teatros. (ver)

7. Cristina y José **leen** _____ en el metro. (leer)

8. Yo **hago** _____ una gira *(tour)* por el centro. (hacer)

10 Una carta de Armando

Complete Armando's letter with the correct forms of the verbs *saber, comer, ver, ir, comprender* and *hacer*.

¡Hola Graciela!

¿(1) **Sabes** _____ tú que Juan y yo estamos en el

Distrito Federal? ¡Es una ciudad fantástica! Al mediodía

nosotros siempre (2) **comemos** _____ mole poblano y

por las tardes (3) **vemos** _____ mucho arte en los

museos. Mañana, yo (4) **voy** _____ a ver a

Óscar. Él (5) **comprende** _____ y habla inglés. ¿Y tú?

¿Cómo estás? ¿Qué (6) **haces** _____ en San

Antonio? ¿(7) **Comes** _____ tacos? Yo

(8) **hago** _____ muchas preguntas, ¿verdad?

Bueno, hasta pronto.

Tu amigo,
Armando

11 ¿Verdad?

Combine elements from each column to write six complete, logical questions with the tag word
verdad.

MODELO Conchita va al colegio, ¿verdad?

Conchita	hacer	una revista
mis amigos	comer	muchas preguntas
yo	ver	inglés y español
tú y Mario	saber	pescado
nosotros	comprender	al colegio
Francisca	leer	el edificio grande
vosotros	ir	mi número de teléfono

Possible answers:

1. **Mis amigos hacen muchas preguntas, ¿verdad?**

   _____

2. **Yo como pescado, ¿verdad?**

   _____

3. **Tú y Mario ven el edificio grande, ¿verdad?**

   _____

4. **Nosotros comprendemos inglés y español, ¿verdad?**

   _____

5. **Francisco lee una revista, ¿verdad?**

   _____

6. **Uds. saben mi número de teléfono, ¿verdad?**

   _____

12 Una carta de México

Imagine you are an exchange student, living with a family in Mexico City. Write a letter to a friend describing your experience. You may use the following outline as a guide.

1. Greet your friend.
2. Say how you are.
3. Tell at what time you go to school and how you get there.
4. Tell what you read in your Spanish class.
5. Mention a food you always eat at school.
6. Mention two things you are going to do on Saturday.
7. Close the letter.

Answers will vary.

Capítulo 4

Lección A

1 La familia Muñoz

Complete the following sentences about the Muñoz family, using the family tree as a reference.

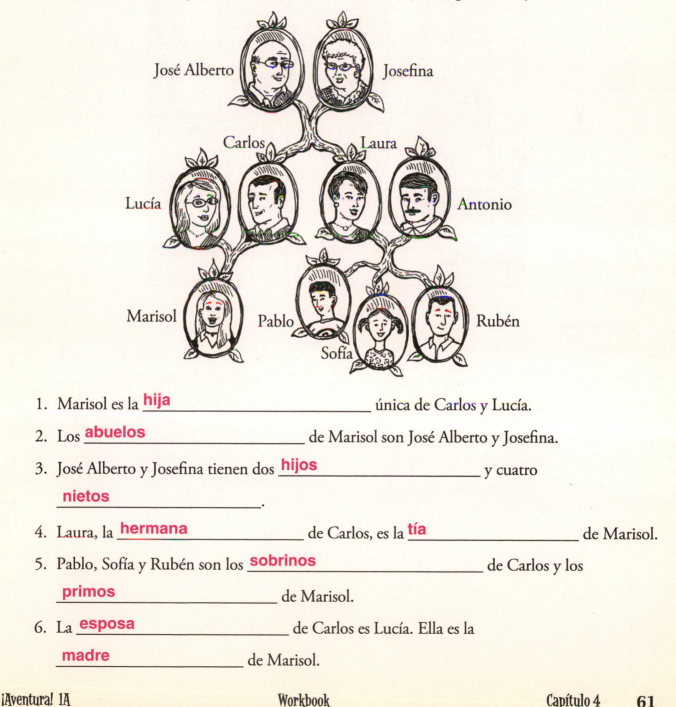

José Alberto   Josefina

Carlos   Laura

Lucía   Antonio

Marisol   Pablo   Sofía   Rubén

1. Marisol es la **hija** _____ única de Carlos y Lucía.

2. Los **abuelos** _____ de Marisol son José Alberto y Josefina.

3. José Alberto y Josefina tienen dos **hijos** _____ y cuatro
   nietos _____ .

4. Laura, la **hermana** _____ de Carlos, es la **tía** _____ de Marisol.

5. Pablo, Sofía y Rubén son los **sobrinos** _____ de Carlos y los
   primos _____ de Marisol.

6. La **esposa** _____ de Carlos es Lucía. Ella es la
   madre _____ de Marisol.

2 Crucigrama

Complete the following crossword puzzle with words you learned in the lesson.

Horizontal

3. El _____ de mi primo es mi tío.

5. El padre de mi padre es mi _____.

6. La familia vive en una _____.

7. El hermano de mi madre es mi _____.

9. El hijo de mi hermana es mi _____.

10. Estamos en Puerto Rico pero _____ en Nueva York.

Vertical

1. El hijo de mis padres es mi _____.

2. Abuelos, tíos, primos son _____.

3. El sobrino de mi madre es mi _____.

4. Mi abuelo es el _____ de mi abuela.

8. Él es hijo _____ porque no tiene hermanos.

3 Puerto Rico

How well do you know Puerto Rico? Match the name of the place in Puerto Rico on the left with the appropriate description in English on the right.

__E__ 1. San Juan   A. the original name of Puerto Rico

__A__ 2. Borinquén   B. popular music in Puerto Rico

__F__ 3. playa de Luquillo   C. a fort built in 1591 to protect the island

__D__ 4. el Yunque   D. a tropical rain forest

__C__ 5. el Castillo de San Felipe del Morro   E. the capital of Puerto Rico

__B__ 6. salsa   F. a beautiful beach

4 Mis primos de Ponce

Rewrite the following sentences, replacing the underlined words with the words in parentheses. Make any necessary changes to the form of the verbs and the adjectives.

> **MODELO**   Mi tía es muy simpática. (mis abuelos)
> Mis abuelos son muy simpáticos.

1. Mi tío favorito vive en Ponce, Puerto Rico. (mis primos)

   Mis primos favoritos viven en Ponce, Puerto Rico.

2. El museo de arte de Ponce es fantástico. (las playas)

   Las playas de Ponce son fantásticas.

3. Hay un restaurante nuevo muy bueno. (una tienda)

   Hay una tienda nueva muy buena.

4. Todos los amigos de mi primo Raúl son divertidos. (las hermanas)

   Todas las hermanas de mi primo Raúl son divertidas.

5. Mi prima es guapa y popular. (mis primos)

   Mis primos son guapos y populares.

6. La casa de mis tíos es grande y bonita. (el carro)

   El carro de mi tío es grande y bonito.

5 Fotos de la familia

Your cousin found an old family album and is wondering who is who in the photographs. Answer her questions in the affirmative, using appropriate possessive adjectives.

> **MODELO** ¿Es ella mi tía?
> <u>Sí, es tu tía.</u>

1. ¿Es ella la abuela de nosotros?

   Sí, es nuestra abuela.

2. ¿Son los hermanos de Ernesto?

   Sí, son sus hermanos.

3. ¿Es el señor el padre de Carolina?

   Sí, es su padre.

4. ¿Son mis primos?

   Sí, son tus primos.

5. ¿Es la señora guapa tu madre?

   Sí, es mi madre.

6. ¿Es él mi sobrino?

   Sí, es tu sobrino.

7. ¿Es el muchacho el primo de nosotros?

   Sí, es nuestro primo.

8. ¿Es ella la esposa de tío Manolo?

   Sí, es su esposa.

9. ¿Son ellos tus hermanos?

   Sí, son mis hermanos.

10. ¿Los señores son los padres de tu madre?

    Sí, son sus padres.

6 Las fotos de José

Help José write labels for the photographs he is putting up on his personal Web site. Complete each phrase with the appropriate possessive adjective.

MODELO   Pedro y <u>su</u> hermana

1. Carmen y ___*sus*___ amigas

2. yo y ___*mi*___ abuelo

3. don Tomás y ___*sus*___ hijos

4. mi amigo y ___*sus*___ parientes

5. nosotros y ___*nuestro*___ profesor

6. el Sr. y la Sra. Ramos y ___*su*___ sobrina

7. yo y ___*mis*___ primos

8. doña Julia y ___*su*___ esposo

7 Mi familia vive en Puerto Rico

Complete the following sentences with the present tense of the verb *vivir*.

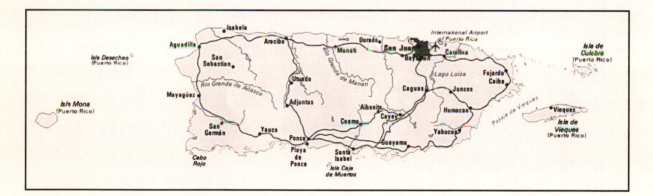

1. Nosotros ___*vivimos*___ en Puerto Rico.

2. Mis abuelos ___*viven*___ en Arecibo.

3. Mi hermano Hernán ___*vive*___ en Mayagüez.

4. Yo ___*vivo*___ en San Juan con mis padres.

5. Mi prima Paulina ___*vive*___ en Ponce.

6. Mis tíos ___*viven*___ en Fajardo.

7. ¿Y tú? ¿Dónde ___*vives*___ ?

8 ¡Voy a Puerto Rico!

Enrique is writing an e-mail to a friend. Complete his message with the present tense of the verbs *vivir*, *ir* and *salir*.

| ▼ | Normal ▼ | MIME ▼ | QP 📋 📄 ⬅ 📑 | **Enviar** |

Para: Jorge
De: Enrique
Asunto: ¡Hola!
Cc:

¡Hola!

Estoy en la clase de computación. (1)__**Salgo**_____ a las dos de

la tarde. ¿A qué hora (2)__**sales**_____ tú? ¿Sabes? Mañana yo

(3)__**voy**_____ a ir con mi madre a Puerto Rico. En Puerto

Rico (4)__**viven**_____ mis abuelos. Ellos (5)__**viven**_____

muy cerca de la playa. Nosotros (6)__**vamos**_____ en avión

porque (7)__**vivimos**_____ en Nueva York y Puerto Rico está lejos.

El avión (8)__**sale**_____ a las diez de la mañana. Mi hermano

no (9)__**va**_____ porque él estudia en España. Él

(10)__**vive**_____ en Barcelona con un primo de mi padre.

Ellos siempre están en casa: no (11)__**salen**_____ de Barcelona.

¿Y tú? ¿Jorge (12)__**vas**_____ a ir a otra ciudad en el verano?

　　　Enrique

9 ¿Cómo está?

Match the situation in English on the left with the appropriate expression in Spanish on the right. Write the letter of your choice in the space provided.

__C__ 1. Your brother is going to his first job interview.   A. Está triste.

__A__ 2. Sergio's dog just died.   B. Está contento.

__F__ 3. Víctor is wearing a bathing suit to snowboard.   C. Está nervioso.

__B__ 4. Miguel got an A+ on his exam.   D. Está cansado.

__D__ 5. Your uncle worked two night shifts.   E. Está enfermo.

__E__ 6. Your grandfather has the flu.   F. Está loco.

10 No es verdad

Rewrite each of the following sentences, replacing the underlined word with its opposite.

MODELO   Hilda está mal.
Hilda está bien.

1. Nuestra casa está limpia.

    Nuestra casa está sucia.

2. El museo está cerrado hoy.

    El museo está abierto hoy.

3. Humberto está muy contento.

    Humberto está muy triste.

4. Juanita está enferma.

    Juanita está bien.

5. El jugo de naranja está frío.

    El jugo de naranja está caliente.

6. La mesa cerca de la ventana está ocupada.

    La mesa cerca de la ventana está libre.

11 ¿Cómo se llama?

Look at the following wedding announcement and answer the questions.

El día 27 de septiembre, en la iglesia San Vicente Ferrer (Los Dominicos), se efectuó el matrimonio del teniente del Ejército don Mauricio Puebla Sepúlveda y la señorita Caroline Monypenny García.

1. What is the groom's family name? __Puebla__

2. What is the bride's family name? __Monypenny__

3. What is the family name of the groom's mother? __Sepúlveda__

4. What is the family name of the bride's mother? __García__

5. What is Caroline's married name? __Caroline Monypenny de Puebla__

6. In the telephone directory, under what letter will the newlyweds be listed? __P__

12 ¿Cómo están?

Complete the following descriptions with the correct form of *estar* and an appropriate adjective.

MODELO

El pollo <u>está caliente</u>.

1. El parque __está sucio_____ .

2. Los chicos __están apurados_____ .

3. La chica __está enferma_____ .

4. Tú __estás triste_____ .

5. Las ventanas __están abiertas_____ .

6. El estudiante __está nervioso_____ .

7. Mis tíos __están guapos_____ .

8. Nosotros __estamos cansados_____ .

13 Sala de chat

Imagine you are in a chat room talking about your family, real or imaginary. Write six to eight sentences describing your family. Include their names and relationships, where they live, and how they are.

Answers will vary. _____

_____

_____

_____

_____

_____

_____

_____

_____

_____

Lección B

1 Mis nuevos amigos

Imagine you are an exchange student in the Dominican Republic and you write a letter to your parents at home. Complete the letter with the words from the list.

hacer	bailar	escuchar	jugar	gustar
patinar	nadar	tocar	partido	ver

Hola, mamá y papá:

¿Cómo están? Yo estoy bien. Me (1) **gusta** _____ mucho

estudiar en la República Dominicana. Es un país fantástico.

Tengo dos nuevos amigos. Se llaman Rafael y Érica. Son muy simpáticos. A Rafael

le gusta (2) **jugar** _____ al béisbol y

(3) **tocar** _____ el piano. A Érica le gusta

(4) **patinar** _____ sobre ruedas y

(5) **bailar** _____ salsa y merengue. A los dos les

gusta (6) **escuchar** _____ la radio pero no les gusta

(7) **ver** _____ la televisión. Mañana nosotros vamos a

(8) **nadar** _____ en la playa. Y en la tarde, vamos a ir a un

(9) **partido** _____ de béisbol. ¡Qué divertido!

Bueno, hasta luego. Voy a (10) **hacer** _____ la tarea.

Los quiero,

Ricardo

2 ¿Qué te gusta hacer?

Look at each illustration and say whether or not you like doing the activity pictured.

MODELO

Me gusta tocar el piano./No me gusta tocar el piano.

1. **(No) Me gusta jugar al tenis.**

2. **(No) Me gusta hacer la tarea.**

3. **(No) Me gusta ir de**

compras/comprar.

4. **(No) Me gusta escuchar**

la radio.

5. **(No) Me gusta cantar.**

6. **(No) Me gusta nadar.**

7. **(No) Me gusta mirar fotos.**

8. **(No) Me gusta patinar**

sobre ruedas.

3 La República Dominicana

Based on what you have learned about the Dominican Republic, complete the sentences on the left with the phrases on the right.

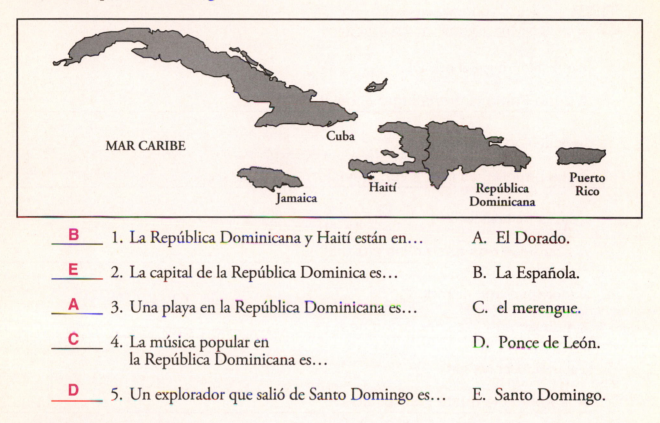

MAR CARIBE   Cuba

Jamaica   Haití   República Dominicana   Puerto Rico

B 1. La República Dominicana y Haití están en…

A. El Dorado.

E 2. La capital de la República Dominica es…

B. La Española.

A 3. Una playa en la República Dominicana es…

C. el merengue.

C 4. La música popular en la República Dominicana es…

D. Ponce de León.

D 5. Un explorador que salió de Santo Domingo es…

E. Santo Domingo.

4 Nos gusta mucho

You and your friends are listing all the things and activities you like about the Dominican Republic. Complete each sentence with either *nos gusta* or *nos gustan*.

1. **Nos gustan** _____ las playas bonitas.

2. **Nos gustan** _____ los partidos de béisbol.

3. **Nos gusta** _____ el merengue.

4. **Nos gustan** _____ los edificios en Santo Domingo.

5. **Nos gusta** _____ ir de compras.

6. **Nos gusta** _____ el Museo de Arte Moderno.

7. **Nos gustan** _____ los parques ecológicos.

8. **Nos gusta** _____ nadar en Boca Chica.

5 ¿Qué les gusta?

Write complete sentences, saying what the following people like to do.

MODELO Selena / contestar en clase
A Selena le gusta contestar en clase.

1. Juan Pablo / jugar al béisbol

   A Juan Pablo le gusta jugar al béisbol.

2. tus amigos / ver televisión

   A tus amigos les gusta ver televisión.

3. nosotros / las ensaladas

   A nosotros nos gustan las ensaladas.

4. tú / los conciertos de rock

   A ti te gustan los conciertos de rock.

5. la abuela / leer revistas

   A la abuela le gusta leer revistas.

6. profesor Bolaños / hacer preguntas

   Al profesor Bolaños le gusta hacer preguntas.

7. yo / los chicos inteligentes

   A mí me gustan los chicos inteligentes.

8. mis hermanos / ir en tren

   A mis hermanos les gusta ir en tren.

6 Conexión dominicana

Read the following profiles of teenagers in the Dominican Republic who are looking for pen pals. Then answer the questions.

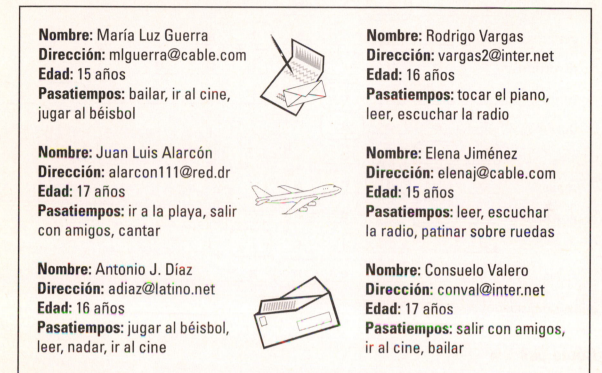

Nombre: María Luz Guerra
Dirección: mlguerra@cable.com
Edad: 15 años
Pasatiempos: bailar, ir al cine, jugar al béisbol

Nombre: Juan Luis Alarcón
Dirección: alarcon111@red.dr
Edad: 17 años
Pasatiempos: ir a la playa, salir con amigos, cantar

Nombre: Antonio J. Díaz
Dirección: adiaz@latino.net
Edad: 16 años
Pasatiempos: jugar al béisbol, leer, nadar, ir al cine

Nombre: Rodrigo Vargas
Dirección: vargas2@inter.net
Edad: 16 años
Pasatiempos: tocar el piano, leer, escuchar la radio

Nombre: Elena Jiménez
Dirección: elenaj@cable.com
Edad: 15 años
Pasatiempos: leer, escuchar la radio, patinar sobre ruedas

Nombre: Consuelo Valero
Dirección: conval@inter.net
Edad: 17 años
Pasatiempos: salir con amigos, ir al cine, bailar

1. ¿A quién le gusta tocar el piano?

   A Rodrigo le gusta tocar el piano.

2. ¿A quiénes les gusta leer?

   A Antonio, Rodrigo y Elena les gusta leer.

3. ¿Qué le gusta hacer a Consuelo?

   A Consuelo le gusta salir con amigos, ir al cine y bailar.

4. ¿A quiénes les gusta jugar al béisbol?

   A María Luz y a Antonio les gusta jugar al béisbol.

5. ¿Le gusta bailar a Juan Luis?

   No, a Juan Luis no le gusta bailar.

6. ¿A ti qué te gusta hacer?

   Answers will vary.

7 Juego

Write the opposite words in the spaces provided. Then unscramble the circled letters to complete the sentence on the bottom.

1. rápido   l   e   (n)   t   o

2. generosa   e   g   o   í   s   (t)   a

3. divertido   a   b   u   (r)   r   i   d   o

4. tonto   i   n   t   (e)   l   i   g   e   n   (t)   e

5. bonitos   f   e   o   (s)

6. alta   b   (a)   j   a

7. mala   b   u   (e)   n   a

8. gordo   d   (e)   l   g   a   d   o

9. fácil   d   i   f   í   c   (i)   l

10. rubia   m   o   r   e   (n)   a

La clase de español es **interesante** .

8 ¿Cómo es?

Complete the following descriptions, according to the pictures.

MODELO

Alicia es <u>baja.</u>

1. Raquel es **alta** .

2. Don Fernando es **calvo** .

3. El avión es **rápido** .

4. La clase es **aburrida** .

5. Quique es **cómico** .

6. La tarea es **difícil** .

9 ¿Qué quiere decir?

Match the description in English on the left with the correct expression in Spanish on the right.

___D___ 1. The fruit is not ripe.　　　A. Está guapa.

___A___ 2. Marta looks pretty today.　　B. Es en el parque.

___F___ 3. Marta is at the park.　　　C. Es guapa.

___C___ 4. Marta is pretty.　　　　　D. Está verde.

___E___ 5. Marta's backpack is green.　E. Es verde.

___B___ 6. The concert is in the park.　F. Está en el parque.

10 ¿Cuál es el verbo correcto?

Circle the verb that logically completes each sentence.

1. Mi padre (**es** / está) un señor bueno, inteligente y generoso.

2. Lorenzo va a ir al médico porque (es / **está**) enfermo.

3. Mis hermanos y yo (**somos** / estamos) de Nueva York.

4. ¿Dónde (**es** / está) el concierto de Marc Anthony?

5. ¿Por qué (eres / **estás**) nerviosa, Lita?

6. La casa de Juan (es / **está**) cerca de la playa.

11 *¿Ser o estar?*

Complete the following conversation with the correct forms of the verbs *ser* or *estar*.

MARTÍN: ¡Hola, Berta! ¿Cómo (1)__estás__?

BERTA: Bien, gracias. Oye, (2)__estás__ muy guapo.

MARTÍN: Gracias. Voy a una fiesta.

BERTA: ¿Sí? ¿Dónde (3)__es__ la fiesta?

MARTÍN: En la casa de Lorena.

BERTA: ¿Quién (4)__es__ Lorena?

MARTÍN: Lorena (5)__es__ la prima de Carlos. Ella (6)__está__ en nuestra clase

de computación. (7)__Es__ de la República Dominicana.

BERTA: (8)__Es__ la chica alta, delgada y morena, ¿verdad?

MARTÍN: Sí. ¿Quieres ir a la fiesta?

BERTA: No, gracias. (9)__Estoy__ ocupada.

12 Hay un concierto

Look at the following advertisement for a concert. Use the information in it to answer the questions.

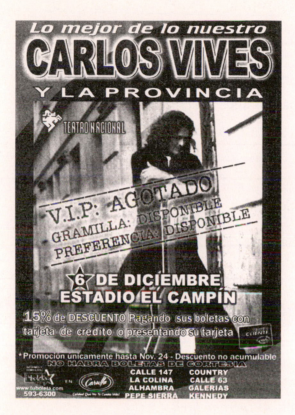

1. ¿Cuándo es el concierto?

   El concierto es el 6 de diciembre.

2. ¿Dónde es el concierto?

   Es en el Estadio El Campín.

3. ¿Quién es el cantante?

   El cantante es Carlos Vives.

4. ¿Cómo es él? ¿Moreno o rubio?

   Él es moreno (y alto).

5. ¿Te gusta ir a conciertos? ¿Por qué?

   Possible answer: Sí, me gusta ir a conciertos porque son divertidos.

13 Mi pariente favorito

Answer the following questions about your favorite relative, real or imaginary.

1. ¿Quién es tu pariente favorito?

   Answers will vary. _____

   _____

2. ¿Cómo se llama? ¿Cuántos años tiene?

   _____

   _____

3. ¿De dónde es? ¿Dónde vive?

   _____

   _____

4. ¿Cómo es su físico *(physical appearance)*?

   _____

   _____

5. ¿Cómo es su personalidad *(personality)*?

   _____

   _____

6. ¿Qué le gusta hacer?

   _____

   _____

7. ¿Qué cosas *(things)* no le gustan?

   _____

   _____

8. ¿Cómo estás cuando ves a tu pariente favorito? ¿Por qué?

   _____

   _____

Capítulo 5

Lección A

1 En la tienda

Complete the following sentences logically with the appropriate words.

lástima	casete	equipo	dinero	reproductor
disco	quemador	aparatos	caramba	canción

1. Los chicos entran en la tienda de __aparatos__ electrónicos.

2. Mauricio busca el __disco__ compacto con la nueva __canción__ de Marc Anthony.

3. ¡__Caramba__! La tienda no tiene el CD, solamente *(only)* tiene el __casete__.

4. Carolina ve un __equipo__ de sonido, un __reproductor__ de MP3 y un __quemador__ de CDs.

5. ¡Qué __lástima__! Ella no tiene __dinero__ para comprar los aparatos.

2 Costa Rica

Read the following statements about Costa Rica. If the statement is true, write **T** in the space provided. If the statement is false, write **F**.

___T___ 1. Costa Rica means "rich coast."

___F___ 2. Costa Rica is the largest and most populous country in Central America.

___T___ 3. Costa Rica has had no army for more than fifty years.

___F___ 4. Costa Rica is a flat country.

___F___ 5. *Irazú* is a beautiful beach.

___T___ 6. Costa Rica is famous for its ecological tourism.

3 ¿Qué tienen?

What do the following people have in their suitcases as they leave on a trip to Costa Rica? Complete the sentences with the present tense of the verb *tener*.

1. Arturo **tiene** _____ un mapa de Costa Rica.

2. Nosotros **tenemos** _____ tres discos compactos de música salsa.

3. Irene y Maite **tienen** _____ cinco camisetas.

4. Tú **tienes** _____ un diccionario de español.

5. Yo **tengo** _____ dos libros sobre las selvas tropicales.

6. Don César **tiene** _____ mucho dinero.

4 ¡Qué sorpresa!

What a coincidence! Write a sentence saying that the person in parentheses also has it. Be sure to change the verb forms when necessary.

MODELO Guillermo tiene veinte años. (yo)
Yo también tengo veinte años.

1. El Sr. Camacho tiene un reproductor de MP3. (mis primos)

   Mis primos también tienen un reproductor de MP3.

2. Yo tengo tres discos compactos de Santana. (Maricela)

   Maricela también tiene tres discos compactos de Santana.

3. La profesora Ruiz tiene un mapa de San José. (nosotros)

   Nosotros también tenemos un mapa de San José.

4. Lorena tiene un quemador de CDs. (tú)

   Tú también tienes un quemador de CDs.

5. Sergio y Mateo tienen un equipo de sonido japonés. (yo)

   Yo también tengo un equipo de sonido japonés.

6. Mi hermano tiene quince años. (Ramón)

   Ramón también tiene quince años.

5 En el autobús

Imagine you are in a tour bus in Costa Rica. Look at the drawing and write what everyone is holding.

MODELO Daniel
Daniel tiene una revista.

1. Olga

   Olga tiene un reproductor de MP3.

2. los chicos

   Los chicos tienen un mapa (de Costa Rica).

3. Ángela

   Ángela tiene un disco compacto.

4. el Sr. López y Ángela

   El Sr. López y Ángela tienen un periódico.

5. yo

   Yo tengo un libro.

6. tú

   Tú tienes una computadora.

6 ¡Qué país!

While visiting Costa Rica, you are awed by some of its sights. Write an appropriate expression for each situation using *qué* + noun.

> **MODELO** You see *volcán Irazú* with its enormous crater.
> ¡Qué volcán!

1. You go to a large store in Sarchí where they sell colorful, hand-painted wooden carts.

   ¡Qué tienda!

2. You visit the national theater in San José, a beautiful building decorated in rococo style.

   ¡Qué teatro!

3. At Jacó Beach, you run into one of your classmates, who is also visiting Costa Rica.

   ¡Qué sorpresa!

4. You visit Braulio Carrillo, a national park with over 6,000 plant species.

   ¡Qué parque!

5. You watch an interesting movie about Columbus' visit to Puerto Limón.

   ¡Qué película!

6. You see a city bus colorfully decorated with painted murals and lights.

   ¡Qué autobús!

7. You watch an exciting soccer game between Saprissa and Alajuela.

   ¡Qué partido!

8. Tomorrow you go back home. You feel it is a shame that the trip is over.

   ¡Qué lástima!

7 Crucigrama

Complete the following crossword puzzle.

Horizontal

2. No esta semana; la semana que ___.
3. No mucho.
4. Animal que hace miau.
5. Hacer la ___ para ir de viaje.
7. Hay siete días en una ___.
9. Tienda de libros.

Vertical

1. El tenis, el fútbol y el béisbol son ___.
5. ___ en bicicleta.
6. ___ a un amigo por teléfono.
8. La tienda ___ a las 10:00 A.M.

8 Identifica

Circle the verb and underline the direct object in each of the following sentences.

MODELO   Todos los días (llevo) el perro al parque.

1. Víctor (compra) una revista en la librería.

2. El señor Domínguez (hace) las maletas.

3. Tú siempre (escuchas) la radio, ¿verdad?

4. Mis compañeros (ven) la película de Penélope Cruz.

5. La estudiante nueva (contesta) las preguntas del profesor.

6. Todas las mañanas yo (leo) el periódico.

7. Mi tío (toma) el metro cada día.

8. Los ticos (comen) gallo pinto.

9. Doña Rosita (hace) un viaje la semana que viene.

9 La *a personal*

Write the *a personal* only in those sentences that require it.

1. Mi padre tiene __—__ tres hermanos y una hermana.

2. Yo veo __a__ mi tío Antonio cada domingo.

3. Mi tío tiene __—__ un gato muy gordo.

4. Mi hermana siempre llama __a__ nuestros primos.

5. Ellos escuchan __a__ Shakira.

6. Mis amigos y yo leemos __—__ revistas cómicas.

7. La semana que viene vamos a ver __—__ un partido de tenis.

8. Mi madre lleva __a__ mi hermana al médico.

10 ¿Lo ves?

Look at the drawing and answer the questions, using direct object pronouns.

MODELO ¿Ves el piano?
<u>No, no lo veo.</u>

1. ¿Ves el mapa de Costa Rica? __Sí, lo veo._____

2. ¿Ves la computadora? __No, no la veo._____

3. ¿Ves el reproductor de DVDs? __Sí, lo veo._____

4. ¿Ves los libros? __Sí, los veo._____

5. ¿Ves el equipo de sonido? __No, no lo veo._____

6. ¿Ves las ventanas? __Sí, las veo._____

7. ¿Ves la pizarra? __Sí, la veo._____

8. ¿Ves el dinero? __No, no lo veo._____

9. ¿Ves los pupitres? __Sí, los veo._____

10. ¿Te ves? __No, no me veo._____

11 Complementos directos

Rewrite the following sentences, changing the direct objects nouns to direct object pronous.

> **MODELO**   Graciela lee revistas en español.
> <u>Graciela las lee.</u>

1. Javier tiene el reproductor de CDs.

   Javier lo tiene.

2. Verónica ve a los niños.

   Verónica los ve.

3. No comprendo las palabras.

   No las comprendo.

4. Mario llama a la profesora de inglés.

   Mario la llama.

5. Nosotros tomamos el tren.

   Nosotros lo tomamos.

12 ¿Quién lo hace?

Answer the following questions, using the cues in parentheses and direct object pronouns.

> **MODELO**   ¿Quién llama a Enrique? (el Sr. Garza)
> <u>El Sr. Garza lo llama.</u>

1. ¿Quién compra un reproductor de CDs? (Manuela)

   Manuela lo compra.

2. ¿Quiénes me ven todos los días? (los compañeros)

   Los compañeros te ven todos los días.

3. ¿Quién tiene el CD de Miguel Bosé? (esta tienda)

   Esta tienda lo tiene.

4. ¿Quién te escucha cantar? (el perro)

   El perro me escucha cantar.

5. ¿Quiénes toman jugo de tomate? (Alex y María)

   Alex y María lo toman.

13 La semana que viene

Look at Federico's agenda book and answer the following questions. Use direct object pronouns when appropriate.

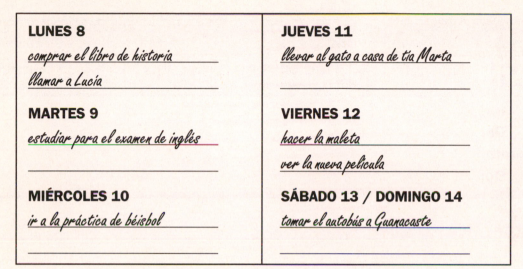

LUNES 8	JUEVES 11
comprar el libro de historia	llevar al gato a casa de tía Marta
llamar a Lucía	
MARTES 9	**VIERNES 12**
estudiar para el examen de inglés	hacer la maleta
	ver la nueva película
MIÉRCOLES 10	**SÁBADO 13 / DOMINGO 14**
ir a la práctica de béisbol	tomar el autobús a Guanacaste

1. ¿Dónde crees (*you think*) que Federico compra el libro de historia?

   Lo compra en una librería.

2. ¿Tiene Federico la práctica de béisbol el martes?

   No, no la tiene el martes.

3. ¿Adónde lleva al gato el jueves?

   Lo lleva a casa de tía Marta.

4. ¿Cuándo va a estudiar inglés?

   El martes lo va a estudiar.

5. ¿Adónde toma el autobús Federico?

   Lo toma a Guanacaste.

6. ¿Cuándo hace la maleta?

   La hace el viernes.

7. ¿Qué día llama Federico a Lucía?

   La llama el lunes.

8. ¿Dónde crees (*you think*) que Federico ve la película el viernes?

   La ve en un cine.

14 ¡Qué viaje!

Imagine you will spend a week in Costa Rica. Write an e-mail to a friend, describing what you will do and see each day of the week.

| | Normal | ▼ | MIME ▼ | QP 🗐 🗐 ▪│ 🗐 | Enviar |

Para:
De:
Asunto:
Cc:

Answers will vary.

_____

_____

_____

_____

_____

_____

_____

_____

_____

Lección B

1 Diciembre

Complete the sentences based on the following calendar.

DICIEMBRE

LUNES	MARTES	MIÉRCOLES	JUEVES	VIERNES	SÁBADO	DOMINGO
	1	2	3	4	5	6
7	8	9	10	11	12	13
14	15	16	17	18	19	20
21	22	23	24	25	26	27
28	29	30	31			

1. Hoy es miércoles 9. ((Ayer) / Mañana) fue martes 8.

2. Hoy es el 31 de diciembre. Mañana es el ((primero de enero) / 30 de diciembre).

3. Hoy es el 17 de diciembre. Anteayer fue el ((15) / 16) de diciembre.

4. Hoy es el veinticinco de diciembre. Es (Noche Vieja / (Navidad)).

5. Mañana es el 11 de diciembre. Hoy es ((jueves) / viernes).

6. Hoy es lunes 21. Pasado mañana es ((miércoles 23) / jueves 24).

7. Hoy es el 29 de diciembre. ((Anteayer) / Ayer) fue el 27 de diciembre.

8. Mañana es Noche Vieja. Hoy es el (24 / (30)) de diciembre.

2 Un cumpleaños especial

Complete the following paragraph with the words from the list.

| mayor | mucho | fue | viene | veintitrés |
| cumpleaños | temprano | fantástico | nueve | celebrarlo |

Ayer, (1)__veintitrés_____ de noviembre, (2)__fue_____

mi (3)__cumpleaños_____. Para (4)__celebrarlo_____, mis amigos

y yo fuimos al concierto de Ricardo Montaner. Todos los años Ricardo Montaner

(5)__viene_____ a nuestra ciudad. Me gustan

(6)__mucho_____ sus canciones. Mi hermana

(7)__mayor_____ de 19 años también fue al concierto. Fue a las

(8)__nueve_____ de la noche pero llegamos al Estadio Nacional

(9)__temprano_____, a las siete y media. ¡Fue (10)__fantástico_____!

3 Nicaragua

Write each letter labeled on the map next to the corresponding description of the place.

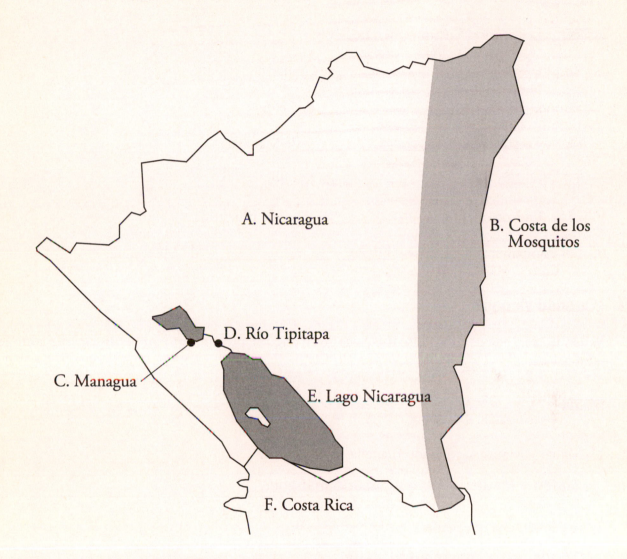

____F____ 1. Nicaragua's neighbor to the south.

____A____ 2. The largest country in Central America.

____C____ 3. Nicaragua's capital and largest commercial center.

____D____ 4. River connecting Lake Managua and Lake Nicaragua.

____E____ 5. The only freshwater lake in the world to have sharks.

4 ¿De dónde vienen?

Everyone in the tour group visited a different place in Nicaragua. Complete the following
sentences with the present tense of **venir** to find out where everyone comes from.

MODELO   Los señores Castro <u>vienen</u> de Rivas.

1. Yo ___**vengo**_____ de Granada.

2. Samuel ___**viene**_____ de León.

3. Flor y Laura ___**vienen**_____ de Managua.

4. Tú ___**vienes**_____ de Masaya.

5. El Sr. Quiroga ___**viene**_____ de Bluefields.

6. Los compañeros de Tobías ___**vienen**_____ de Matagalpa.

5 ¿Cuándo vienen?

When is everyone coming? Use the clues given and the present tense of **venir** to write complete
sentences.

MODELO   José / mañana
José viene mañana.

1. Mateo y Mauricio / pasado mañana

Mateo y Mauricio vienen pasado mañana.

2. tú / la semana que viene

Tú vienes la semana que viene.

3. nosotros / el primero de enero

Nosotros venimos el primero de enero.

4. Hortensia / hoy

Hortensia viene hoy.

5. mis parientes / el fin de semana

Mis parientes vienen el fin de semana.

6 ¿Cómo vienen a la fiesta?

Look at the illustrations and write complete sentences, telling how everyone is arriving to the party.

MODELO Alberto

Alberto viene en moto.

1. Raúl

Raúl viene en taxi.

2. Sara y Rosa

Sara y Rosa vienen en tren.

3. Dolores

Dolores viene a pie.

4. nosotros

Nosotros venimos en autobús.

5. tú

Tú vienes en bicicleta.

6. Doña Julia

Doña Julia viene en carro.

7. mis primos

Mis primos vienen en barco.

8. yo

Yo vengo en avión.

7 Doce meses

In the word-square below, find and circle the Spanish names for the twelve months of the year.
The words may read horizontally, vertically or diagonally.

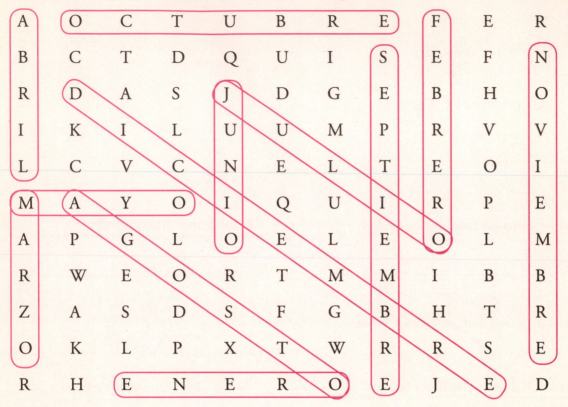

A	O	C	T	U	B	R	E	F	E	R
B	C	T	D	Q	U	I	S	E	F	N
R	D	A	S	J	D	G	E	B	H	O
I	K	I	L	U	U	M	P	R	V	V
L	C	V	C	N	E	L	T	E	O	I
M	A	Y	O	I	Q	U	I	R	P	E
A	P	G	L	O	E	L	E	O	L	M
R	W	E	O	R	T	M	M	I	B	B
Z	A	S	D	S	F	G	B	H	T	R
O	K	L	P	X	T	W	R	R	S	E
R	H	E	N	E	R	O	E	J	E	D

8 ¿Cuánto es?

Read the following numbers and write them out, using numerals.

MODELO   mil setecientos   <u>1.700</u>

1. trescientos veinticinco   <u>**325**</u>

2. cien mil novecientos dos   <u>**100.902**</u>

3. mil cuatrocientos cincuenta   <u>**1.450**</u>

4. cinco mil ciento veintidós   <u>**5.122**</u>

5. doscientos cuarenta mil ochocientos once   <u>**240.811**</u>

6. novecientos noventa mil quinientos uno   <u>**990.501**</u>

7. setecientos mil cuatrocientos quince   <u>**700.415**</u>

8. cien mil, ciento trece   <u>**100.113**</u>

9 Contesta

Answer the following questions.

1. ¿Cuál es la fecha de hoy? **Answers will vary.**

   _____

2. ¿Cuándo es el cumpleaños de tu mejor amigo(a)?

   _____

3. ¿Cuántos años cumple tu amigo(a)? ¿Es joven o viejo?

   _____

4. ¿En qué fecha es el Día de Año Nuevo?

   _____

5. ¿Qué año va a ser? ¿Te gusta la idea de estar en ese año?

   _____

6. ¿Pasan los años rápidamente?

   _____

10 Los días de fiesta

Complete each statement, using your knowledge of holidays throughout the Spanish-speaking world.

__C__ 1. El Día de San Valentín es…   A. el treinta y uno de diciembre.

__F__ 2. El Día del Trabajo es…   B. el veinticuatro de diciembre.

__A__ 3. La Noche Vieja es…   C. el catorce de febrero.

__G__ 4. El Día de los Inocentes es…   D. el seis de enero.

__B__ 5. La Nochebuena es…   E. el primero de enero.

__D__ 6. El Día de los Reyes Magos es…   F. el primero de mayo.

__J__ 7. El Día de la Raza es…   G. el veintiocho de diciembre.

__I__ 8. La Navidad es…   H. el primero de noviembre.

__H__ 9. El Día de Todos los Santos es…   I. el veinticinco de diciembre.

__E__ 10. El Día de Año Nuevo es…   J. el doce de octubre.

11 ¿Cuánto cuesta?

Look at the following newspaper ad for electronics.
Then answer the questions, spelling out the numbers.

`MODELO` ¿Cuánto cuesta el microcomponente?
Cuesta ciento cuarenta y nueve mil novecientos.

1. ¿Cuánto cuesta el reproductor DVDs?

Cuesta ciento veintinueve

mil novecientos.

_____

2. ¿Cuánto cuesta el video grabador?

Cuesta noventa y nueve

mil novecientos.

_____

3. ¿Cuánto cuesta el equipo Sony MHC-RG22?

Cuesta ciento cuarenta y nueve

mil novecientos.

_____

4. ¿Cuánto cuesta el equipo Sony MHC-RG33?

Cuesta ciento sesenta y nueve

mil novecientos.

_____

Microcomponente SONY CMT-M70, reproductor de CD, 20 W RMSx2, modos DSGx2, sintonizador digital con memoria para 30 emisoras (20 FM/10AM), Deck full logic, control remoto
Cod. 1804130
Antes $ 179.900 Ahora $ 149.900

Equipo Sony MHC-RG22. 1300W PMPO, cambiador de 3 CD, Game Sync, ecualizador directo de audio/video, parlante de 3 vías
Cod. 1805446
$ 149.900

Video grabador modelo SLV-LX 77, VHS 6 cabezales Hi-Fi, stereo con sintonizador MTS máxima resolución, búsqueda de programas con perilla, sistema TRILOGIC, cabezales de 19 micrones
cod.1802046
$ 99.900

Reproductor DVD modelo DVP-NS315, Virtual Surround Sonidos envolventes utilizando sólo altavoces de TV, reproduce CD-R/RW/Lectura MP3, reductor de ruidos en líneas verticales.
Cod. 1803091
Antes $ 149.900 Ahora $ 129.900

Equipo Sony MHC-RG33. 1700W PMPO, cambiador de 3 CD, gabinete hexagonal, Game Sync. ecualizador directo de audio/video, parlante de 3 vías
Cod. 1805442
Antes $ 189.900 Ahora $ 169.900

12 Fechas históricas

Spell out the dates of the following historical dates in Latin American history.

> **MODELO**   Nicaragua declara la independencia de España: 15/9/1821
> _el quince de septiembre de mil ochocientos veintiuno_

1. Cristóbal Colón llega a Cuba: 27/10/1492

   el veintisiete de octubre de mil cuatrocientos noventa y dos

2. Hernán Cortés toma la capital de los aztecas: 13/08/1521

   el trece de agosto de mil quinientos veintiuno

3. México declara la independencia de España: 16/09/1810

   el dieciséis de septiembre de mil ochocientos diez

4. La Universidad de San Marcos en Perú abre: 12/05/1551

   el doce de mayo de mil quinientos cincuenta y uno

5. El huracán Mitch llega a Centroamérica: 31/10/1998

   el treinta y uno de octubre de mil novecientos noventa y ocho

6. Gabriel García Márquez recibe el Premio Nóbel de Literatura: 08/12/1982

   el ocho de diciembre de mil novecientos ochenta y dos

7. Crean la Organización de Estados Americanos: 30/04/1948

   el treinta de abril de mil novecientos cuarenta y ocho

8. El astronauta costarricense Franklin Chang-Díaz va al espacio: 12/01/1986

   el doce de enero de mil novecientos ochenta y seis

13 Mi cumpleaños

Write a paragraph in which you say when your birthday is, how old you will be, and whether you like the idea of turning that age a lot or not even a little bit. Also mention who is coming to your birthday and describe your plans for that day.

Answers will vary. _____

_____

_____

_____

_____

_____

_____

_____

_____

_____

_____

_____

_____

_____

_____

_____

_____

_____